M000217968

THE WHEATLEY
DIARY

Other Military Books published by The Windrush Press
The Recollections of Rifleman Harris
   Edited and Introduced by Christopher Hibbert
The Letters of Private Wheeler
   Edited and with a Foreword by B.H. Liddell Hart
The Diaries of a Napoleonic Foot Soldier
   Edited and Introduced by Mark Raeff
A Soldier of the 71st
   Edited and Introduced by Christopher Hibbert

Titles in the GREAT BATTLES series
Hastings by Peter Poyntz Wright
Agincourt by Christopher Hibbert
Edgehill: 1642 by Peter Young
Corunna by Christopher Hibbert
Wellington's Peninsular Victories by Michael Glover
Trafalgar: The Nelson Touch by David Howarth
Waterloo: A Near Run Thing by David Howarth

EDMUND WHEATLEY
A Self-Portrait

THE WHEATLEY
DIARY

*A Journal and Sketch-book
kept during the
Peninsular War and the
Waterloo Campaign*

EDITED WITH
AN INTRODUCTION AND NOTES BY
CHRISTOPHER HIBBERT

THE WINDRUSH PRESS · GLOUCESTERSHIRE

First published in Great Britain by Longmans, Green and Co. Ltd, 1964
Reprinted in 1997 by The Windrush Press
Little Window,
High Street, Moreton-in-Marsh,
Gloucestershire GL56 0LL
Telephone: 01608 652012
Fax: 01608 652125

British Library Cataloguing in Publication Data
A catalogue record for this book is available from the British Library

ISBN 1 900624 06 0

The painting on the front cover is a self-portrait of
Edmund Wheatley 'skulking like an outlaw in a thicket'

Printed and bound in Great Britain by
Bell & Bain Ltd., Glasgow

Contents

Illustrations

PLATES

Maps

Introduction
by Christopher Hibbert

'About one o'clock in the morning I was reading in my tent when who should come in but Llewellyn. Surprised at this early visit and more so when he enquired where the Sentry was and said that no body was round the fire, out I sallied with a candle and found the Sentry dead drunk and Corporal Einer insensible by the fire with one man, and the other man missing. All the kicking possible could not revive them and I was obliged to stand Sentry myself till day break, Llewellyn cooking the coffee.

'On arousing Corporal Einer, I discovered a couple of muleteers had been treating them with aqua dentae, a bottle of which I discovered under some furze.... And after a fatiguing search, I found [the missing man] in a bush stripped naked and frozen to death.

'Not knowing how to conceal this unpleasant business from the Colonel (as death to them all is the result of sleeping upon duty before the enemy, and having once been guilty of the same offence myself) I determined to screen the poor fellows. So digging a deep hole we buried the man and I reported him as having deserted to the enemy. The other three would go to the Devil for me now. But should it be discovered I shall go to Him myself I fear.'

Edmund Wheatley, who wrote this characteristic entry in his diary on 29 January 1814, was then an ensign in the 5th Line Battalion of the King's German Legion. He was 21 years old and lived in Hammersmith. Though little is known about his career, the diary, which vividly and evocatively describes his experiences during the last stages of the Peninsular War and during the Waterloo campaign, suggests much about his character. He appears in its pages as impetuous, moody, brave and kind, inclined to be argumentative and touchy, often naïve and always likeable. While occasionally allowing himself a fanciful phrase, an introspective thought or a moralizing expression, he disclaims any idea that he is romantic, and he was clearly neither a philosopher nor an introvert. It seems, in fact, that these rather clumsily obtrusive additions to what is otherwise a straightforward narrative of adventure were inserted for the benefit of the young girl to whom the diary is addressed.

This girl, Eliza Brookes, was never far from Wheatley's mind. The diary opens with the mention of a secret assignation with her at Hyde Park Turnpike (at which he was 'not noticed!!!') and it ends with a long protestation of his love for her and his hope that one day the difficulties that stand in the way of their marriage will be overcome. Since these difficulties were well enough known to them both, they are never specifically mentioned; and we can only surmise as to what they were. The strongest hint we have is Wheatley's complaint that 'the obstacle to our happiness is the lack of money'. But it seems that there were other obstacles besides money. Her family had forbidden her to see him or to write to him. 'Not an individual related to you approves of me', he complains sadly. 'Every dissatisfactory object presents itself.'

Perhaps it was his instability that they objected to as much as his poverty. For there can be no doubt that he was recklessly headstrong. It appears that he had already fought a duel with a young man with whom he was at school. And when he returned home from France and was refused leave to go to London, he dashed off to Brighton in a post-chaise where he 'launched out into dissipation' knowing that he would be – as he was – arrested on his return.

Perhaps, also, the Brookes family disapproved of Eliza's choice because whereas they might have forgiven the wild escapades of a penniless young officer in the Household Cavalry or the Foot Guards, they found the same behaviour far more reprehensible in a subaltern in a line battalion of the King's German Legion.

The Legion had been in existence for only nine years when Wheatley was ('without purchase') gazetted Ensign in November 1812 and joined its depot at Bexhill.[1] And despite the distinguished service of various of its regiments – particularly its cavalry regiments – it was at that time considered an unsuitable corps for an English gentleman to join.

Most of its officers were Germans who had come over to England after Napoleon had overrun Hanover in 1803 and had disbanded the Electoral army. In Wheatley's battalion there was, in fact (apart from the paymaster), only one other British officer, the companionable Henry Llewellyn, a portrait of whose 'drunken face' appears in this diary in Plate 11.

Although the officers of the Legion were nearly all Germans, however, many of their men were not, and the corps had consequently lost much of its original Hanoverian flavour and discipline. From the first it had admittedly been designed as a depository for men of all the nations of Europe – except France, Italy and Spain – willing to fight in the war against Napoleon. But the early recruits had been for the most part Hanoverians; while the great numbers of other Hanoverians that had been enlisted when the Legion was serving in North Germany as part of Lord Cathcart's expedition in 1805 had not only increased their preponderance, but had so enlarged the Legion that its complement was raised to eight battalions of light infantry, two regiments of dragoons, three regiments of light dragoons as well as artillery and engineers. In later years, though, when connexions with the Electorate were completely severed, it had been found impossible to maintain the strength of this large corps without recourse to numerous less desirable recruits from other parts of Germany and from eastern Europe. The

1. War Office Records.

Legion's ranks became filled with Poles, Illyrians, Hungarians and Russians as well as Danes, Swedes, Dutchmen and Germans of all sorts. Many of them volunteered only to escape from prisoner-of-war camps or to avoid going to jail; and as soon as they left on active service, with no particular sense of loyalty either to their regiment or to the country it served, showed little interest in anything other than drink, women, plunder and the possibilities of desertion.

The various units of the Legion, nevertheless, continued to perform a worthwhile and often valuable service. They were in the expeditionary force which laid siege to Copenhagen in 1807; they had taken part in the Walcheren expedition as well as in the expedition to the Weser and in the invasion of Italy; they had served in the Peninsula under Sir John Moore during the Corunna campaign of 1808; had followed Sir Arthur Wellesley into Spain in the summer of 1809 and had fought bravely in the subsequent battles of Talavera, Barosa and Albuera. Since August 1812 'in consideration of the King's German Legion having so frequently distinguished themselves against the enemy, and particularly upon the occasion of the late victory obtained near Salamanca', its officers had been granted permanent rank in the British Army.[1]

There was, nevertheless, a feeling in the Army, and to a lesser extent in the country as a whole, that the credit for the continued reputation of the Legion belonged more to its undoubtedly skilful and dashing cavalry regiments than to its infantry battalions. To some extent the opinion was justified. But so long as he could rely on the faithful and dedicated service of those fine German officers who were still to be found in every battalion, Wellington was prepared to consider the Legion's infantry as being amongst his most trustworthy troops.

Edmund Wheatley, who considered them from a somewhat different standpoint, while no doubt sharing the Commander-in-Chief's high opinion of some of these officers, found few of them satisfactory companions.

He seems to have made no close friends in his own battalion other than Llewellyn, and apparently spent his leisure hours, when he could, with Englishmen who were officers in other units in his brigade – Lieutenants Alexander Carmichael, George Boyd and William Drysdale of the 1st Line Battalion K.G.L., Ensign John Henderson of the K.G.L. Artillery, and Charles Beverley, a Deputy Assistant Commissary-General, who enrages Wheatley the day before the Battle of Waterloo by allowing his 'fiery horse' to 'prance' mud in his face, 'by which manoeuvre', Wheatley indignantly adds, 'my military hat fell in the mud, [out of which] dropped

1. War Office Order, 10 August 1812, quoted by North Ludlow Beamish, *History of the King's German Legion*, ii (1837), 86. A more recent history than Beamish's is Bernhard Schwertfeger's *Geschichte der Königlich Deutschen Legion 1803–1816* (Hanover and Leipzig, 1907). See also the article by Lieutenant-Colonel R. E. F. G. North, 'The Raising and Organizing of the K.G.L.', in the *Journal of the Society for Army Historical Research* (December 1961).

my night Cap and some brown bread which were completely soaked'.
Captain Nötting, his Company Commander, Wheatley detests. Whereas
the other German officers in the battalion are rarely even so much as mentioned, Nötting appears regularly and nearly always to be insulted. Variously
described as 'bullying', 'spiteful', and a 'rascal' full of 'german malice' and
'dastardly enmity', Nötting is presented as the thoroughgoing villain of the
5th Battalion. He constantly provokes Wheatley to retorts which seem so
unpardonable in a junior officer that we may suspect them to have been
heightened by *l'esprit d'escalier*. Once, for instance, limping back to the
battalion after a day's hard fighting, utterly exhausted and not yet recovered
from a wound inflicted some weeks before, Wheatley is greeted by Nötting's
cry, 'Well, Sir, I thought you had deserted!'
'Your thoughts, sir, like yourself,' he answers, 'are good for nothing.'
Two months later Wheatley is defending a house which is being gradually
demolished by French cannon during the siege of Bayonne – Wheatley's
account of this, incidentally, is one of the very few first-hand narratives of the
operation that exist and is by far the most vivid. He loses ten men, and eventually the roof of the room from which he is returning the fire with Lather,
the Company's shoemaker, collapses over their heads.
'The Shoemaker's head was actually scalped,' he relates. 'And when I
groped out into the yard like a miller, the Captain says, "I thought you was
killed, Wheatley. Where is the Company?"
' "You will see them again," I answered, "and I hope shortly."
' "Why, where are they, then, sir?"
' "Gone to hell!" '
For his Colonel, Baron Ompteda, however, Wheatley obviously has a
high respect. Only once does he make a direct comment on him. This is
during the Battle of the Nivelle. Wheatley has just seen his friend Boyd
killed by a musket ball that struck the back of his head 'and passed out
between the eyes'. Shocked and with a lacerated foot, he loses his way on
returning to the battalion, which he finds has been relieved by the 2nd
Battalion. He sees Llewellyn sitting down and talking to Colonel Ompteda
and the Baron's two young nephews and he joins the group.
'Although I did not relish the cannon balls now and then tearing the
earth about us,' he comments, 'I saw no change in the Colonel's countenance
and he laughed and joked his little nephew for holding his breath as they
flew over us like a passing whirlwind.'
That night Wheatley feels so cold while on battalion guard that he rolls
himself in his sergeant's blanket and sleeps at the foot of a tree.
He is woken by a 'violent kick in the neck' and the Colonel's angry voice.
But later in the night the Colonel apologizes for kicking him and walks up
and down with him for an hour, talking to him to keep him awake, as
together they watch the fires burning beside the French batteries.
But although Wheatley gives no other indication of his respect for

Baron Ompteda, the reader cannot fail to share the young man's shock and sadness when after the suicidal charge at Waterloo, which Ompteda should never have been ordered to make, Wheatley regains consciousness, having been wounded in the head, to find his Colonel lying beside him in a ditch 'his head stretched back with his mouth open, and a hole in his throat'.

A Frenchman's arm is lying across his leg, Wheatley tells us, and he is so confused that he does not remember where he is for the moment. But then he sees the backs of some French soldiers and remembers. He hears French voices close at hand and pretends to be dead. He feels someone tug at his epaulettes and realizing that the man will soon turn him over to rifle his pockets, he leaps up and tries to run away. But dizziness overcomes him and he begins to fall when the French soldier grasps his collar, 'grinning, "*Ou va's tu chien?*"'

He begs the soldier to allow him to regain his cap, for which throughout the diary he displays a high and touching regard, and, having been granted this request, he is pushed inside the farmhouse of La Haye Sainte, where his truly horrifying experiences as a prisoner of war begin.

In recalling these various incidents I hope I have been able to convey something of the atmosphere of this remarkable little book. Wheatley's diary does not add much of importance to our general knowledge of the campaigns in which he fought – though many new details are supplied, particularly about the fighting outside Bayonne – but it does give an extraordinarily vivid impression of what it was like to be in Wellington's army, of how men lived and died, what they saw and felt and endured.

Most of the firsthand English accounts of the Napoleonic Wars that have come down to us were written long after the events they describe. The first half of Wheatley's diary was written at the time – 'abroad in all weathers', as he puts it himself – and the second half, which deals with the Waterloo campaign and is no less vivid, within two years.

Also, Wheatley's is one of the very few accounts of life in the King's German Legion available in English. The best known of these is the diary of August Schaumann which was translated into English as *On the Road with Wellington* in 1924. But throughout the period covered by Wheatley, Schaumann was serving as commissary with an English regiment. The anonymous author of *Journal of an Officer in the King's German Legion* (1827) was on the medical staff of the Legion throughout his service, but he did not serve in Wheatley's campaigns. Baron Ompteda, a memoir of whose life based on his letters to his brother was written by his nephew and published in English in 1892, did, of course, see the same scenes that Wheatley saw; but his writing is very colourless and his letters are much concerned with family affairs.

Wheatley was, perhaps, a better stylist as a draughtsman than as a writer; but his capacity to bring a scene to life is little hampered by his scant regard for the rules of syntax and his entire rejection of the uses of punctuation.

To make his diary easier to read I have given it the punctuation and paragraphs it entirely lacks; and where the sense is, on first reading, somewhat obscure I have added a word or phrase and placed it in square brackets. [*My own explanations and interpolations are also placed between square brackets and in italics like this.*] Otherwise I have not tampered with the text, except to write out words in full whenever Wheatley has abbreviated them (as he frequently does), to rearrange the position of some of the descriptive entries so that the narrative parts of the diary run on without interruption, and to omit a few of the rather tedious passages in which he reflects upon metaphysical subjects. His sometimes curious spelling has been preserved (except in the case of proper names) as has been his erratic use of capital letters, though obvious slips of the pen – a word is often duplicated – have been corrected.

The diary is written in faded sepia ink on 277 small sheets of paper and has been bound between leather-covered boards. Interspersed in the text are pen-and-wash drawings and water-colours which have been reproduced in the following pages. The diary was handed to my publishers by the late Wallis Goslett, Edmund Wheatley's great-great-grandson, whose help and interest were most encouraging.

I want also to thank Mrs Joan St George Saunders of Writers' and Speakers' Research for her help in collecting information about Edmund Wheatley's subsequent career, my friend Major Freddie Myatt, M.C., for putting his wide knowledge of military life during the Peninsular period at my disposal, my wife for her help in compiling the index, Mr Hamish Francis and the Hon. Georgina Stonor.

*

When the diary opens in the summer of 1813, Wellington's new campaign is going well. The previous year, taking advantage of Napoleon's preoccupation with Russia, the British Commander had advanced southwards from his winter quarters in Portugal to Badajoz, which, with the loss of 5,000 men, he had captured in April 1812. Marching north again and then east across Spain, he defeated Marshal Marmont at Salamanca and the day after the battle the First Regiment of Dragoons in the King's German Legion wiped out two regiments of Foy's rearguard in what that General thought was the most brilliant cavalry attack made in the whole of the Peninsular War. By the middle of August, Wellington was in Madrid; and a month later, having turned north again, he was laying siege to Burgos.

But at Burgos the triumphs of 1812 came to an end and before the year was out the British army, hungry, tired and dispirited, was retreating once more across the cold wastes of central Spain.

The campaign of 1813, however, had so far been unclouded by any such disaster. In brilliant summer sunshine the refreshed and reinforced army had advanced quickly through the Tras-os-Montes and Old Castile, and the French had fallen back before them, evacuating Valladolid, Palencia and Burgos, all in the first fortnight of June. Then, having crossed the Ebro on 15 June, the cheerful and excited troops had marched on Vitoria, and here six days later they inflicted on the enemy one of the most decisive defeats of the entire war. Fifty thousand of the French managed to escape by way of Pamplona and scurried over the Pyrenean passes, but France was at last laid open to attack.

Soon after the end of the month, while Ensign Edmund Wheatley waited at Hilsea Barracks near Portsmouth for his embarkation orders, Wellington came up to the Pyrenees (leaving a force behind him to blockade Pamplona, where the French still held out), and established his left wing under Lieutenant-General Sir Thomas Graham, on the coast near San Sebastian, where the French were also still entrenched.

Under Graham's command at this time was the 1st Division, commanded by Major-General Kenneth Howard. This Division comprised a brigade of Guards (the 1st Battalion 2nd Foot Guards, the 1st Battalion 3rd Foot Guards and a company of the 60th Rifles) commanded by Major-General the Hon. Edward Stopford – a second Guards brigade had remained behind in Portugal owing to sickness – and five battalions of the King's German Legion (the 1st and 2nd Light Battalions and the 1st and 2nd and 5th Line Battalions) commanded by Colonel Colin Halkett.[1] And so it was to the last of these battalions that Wheatley was to go.

Although he went aboard the *Mary* transport on 29 July, however, and was off the Isle of Wight by the morning of 31 July, a storm forced his ship back and on 2 August he was in Plymouth harbour. Meanwhile Wellington had retrieved his army from a dangerous situation.

On 25 July he had been standing in the churchyard at Lesaca waiting for news from San Sebastian which General Graham's storming parties had assaulted at dawn. At eleven o'clock he was told that the attack had failed with heavy losses. Immediately he rode over to the coast to decide what should next be done. On returning to his headquarters at Lesaca, he was met on the road by a messenger who told him that the centre of his line, commanded by Sir Rowland Hill, was under heavy attack.

Marshal Soult, whom Napoleon had sent to Bayonne after the disaster at Vitoria with orders to 're-establish the imperial business in Spain', having pulled the French army together with remarkable speed and efficiency, had resolved on an ambitious plan. Instead of going to the relief of San Sebastian, as Wellington had expected he would, he decided to launch an attack on the

---

1. For the complete order of battle of Wellington's army at this time see Appendix A of *With Wellington in the Pyrenees*, by Major-General F. C. Beatson (1914).

Allied centre and right, to advance to the relief of Pamplona and then sweep round behind Wellington's rear towards the coast.

By 28 July he had almost succeeded. Wellington's subordinates, spread out on so long a front and lost without the guidance of their leader, had felt obliged to fall back almost as far as Pamplona. It was, as Wellington said himself, 'a close run thing'; but galloping south to reach his right wing before Soult attacked it, he arrived in the village of Sorauen, six miles from Pamplona, just in time. Soult was repulsed at Sorauen and when he tried to march across Wellington's flank in an attempt to relieve San Sebastian, his troops were mauled again, and he had no alternative but to retreat once more across the frontier.

By the time Edmund Wheatley had arrived in Spain and settled down with his battalion, Wellington had stabilized his line, San Sebastian had fallen at the second assault and Soult had lost another 4,000 men in a vain attempt to save it.

As soon as he could satisfy himself that the negotiations which Napoleon was carrying on beyond the frontier would not result in strong forces being released to oppose him, Wellington would be ready to take his army across the Bidassoa river into France.

Wheatley's sketch of the positions at Bayonne

The Diary

PART ONE

The Campaign in Southern France, 1813 – 1814

9 August 1813   In Plymouth harbour. Wet and windy.

13 August   In the Bay of Biscay. Mutiny between the Germans and the Irish.[1] Sided with the Germans and seized the ringleaders. Very sick and wretched.

20 August   Disembarked at Pasajes,[2] a small creek surrounded with hills, between San Sebastian and the French frontier. I joined my Battalion [*the 5th Line Battalion K.G.L.*] the same morning and after various changes of position encamped on a lofty Pyrenee with the clouds at times below us. We are on the right of the Madrid road, one mile from a village called Irun[3] situated on the Bidassoa, a small river which separates Spain from France.

1. The Irish were the 27th Regiment (the Inniskilling). Relations between the Irish soldiers and the King's German Legion were never good. In July 1806 when a brigade of the K.G.L. had been stationed at Tullamore there had been serious riots in which several Germans and Irish militiamen had been wounded, two of them mortally. – Beamish, *op. cit.*, i, 95–102.

2. A map showing Wheatley's advances after landing at Pasajes until leaving Tarnos in June 1814 will be found on p. 91.

3. Then an 'exceedingly gloomy, dirty and melancholy-looking place' according to August Schaumann, formerly a lieutenant in the 7th Line Battalion K.G.L., and now a Deputy Assistant Commissary-General with the 18th Hussars. 'Verily he who first enters Spain through Irun must have a fright.' – *On the Road with Wellington: The Diary of a War Commissary in the Peninsular Campaigns*, by August Ludolf Friedrich Schaumann, ed. and trans. Anthony M. Ludovici (Heinemann, 1924), 398.

1

*[The battalion remained in this position, which it strongly fortified, for
several weeks. Wheatley was assigned to the Grenadier Company[1] which
was commanded by Captain George Nötting, the German officer to whom
he was soon to take such a strong dislike.*

*There was little action on either side of the river. Every so often the
Allies sent out a reconnaissance party at night, and sometimes the French
would raid the Allied lines as on the occasion Wheatley now describes.]*

25 September   The French crossed the Bidassoa by night at low water
and crawling a steep hill drove down the Spaniards towards us. But
being weak in numbers they were repulsed at daybreak by the volunteers of Asturias.[2]

This was the first battle I saw and I was delighted at first, but when
crowds of groaning, wounded Spaniards and French prisoners filled
Irun, my look of satisfaction was soon clouded, and a violent reaching
and giddiness was the punishment for enjoying the horrid spectacle of
human butchery with indifference.

It now rained most heavily and after remaining shivering, wet and
cold in the field for about nine hours, I ran [when it was] dark into a
barn full of wounded; [and there I] slept, harrassed, hungry and wet
on some straw with a poor fellow shot in the groins, and on rising
next morn I left him as dead as his musket.

7 October   At one o'clock this morning the dead silence of the Camp
was suddenly changed to a scene of hurry and commotion. A passe-
parole ordered the Companies instantly under arms; and the rattling
of artillery passing soon shook off every drowsy sensation. All was
conjecture and expectation. We supposed the forcing of the river to
be the object.

[They were right. Wellington had learned on 3 September that Austria

1. The grenade had long since gone out of general use in the Army, but battalions
kept their grenadier companies which were considered something of a *corps d'élite*. They
stood on the right of the battalion and wore certain distinctions of uniform, including wings
(metal scales for the officers and worsted for the men) instead of the normal fringed
shoulder epaulette.
2. Wellington had been appointed Generalissimo of the Spanish Armies since the
liberation of Madrid; and there were now over 40,000 Spanish troops under his direct
command. A contributory reason for his reluctance to invade France was his knowledge
that these troops, unpaid and unfed, 'must plunder and will set the whole country against
us'. – *The Despatches of Field Marshal the Duke of Wellington* (1837), xi, 122. The Asturian
Division was commanded by General Juan Diaz Porlier and comprised three battalions. –
Charles Oman, *A History of the Peninsular War*, vi, 753.

2

*had joined Prussia and Russia in war against France, and he had decided
to make an assault on the long line of redoubts that Soult had been building
on the French side of the frontier southwards from Hendaye, and to
advance to the River Nivelle, capturing, on the way, the small port of St
Jean de Luz.*

*For several days he had been cautiously moving unit after unit towards
Irun and Fuenterrabia, along the estuary of the Bidassoa, to reinforce his
left, while Soult, who believed that his adversary would attempt the bolder
plan of encirclement that he himself had attempted in July, was concentrating his reserves at the other end of the thinly held French line opposite
Roncesvalles forty miles to the south-west. Consequently while more than
24,000 Allied troops were assembled at the estuary of the Bidassoa where
Wheatley's battalion stood, there were scarcely more than 10,000 French
troops in their immediate front.*

*These French troops were General Maucune's 7th Division, disposed
along the heights between Hendaye and Biriatou, and Boyer's 9th Division
farther back in Urrugne and south of St Jean de Luz.*

*Wellington's plan of attack was to concentrate the 5th Division around
Fuenterrabia under cover of night, and in the morning to send them wading
across the estuary towards Hendaye, while two miles farther upstream,
the 1st Division, with the K.G.L. battalions on the left and the Guards'
brigade on the right, were to wade through the river opposite Béhobie.*

*The remains of the burned bridge in front of the few houses of Béhobie
can be seen in Wheatley's drawing (Plate 1). This is where his company
was to cross.*

*Lord Aylmer's independent brigade, newly arrived from England, was
to act as support for the 1st Division; while farther upstream the Light
Division and three Spanish divisions were to assault Soult's centre.]*

We remained till daybreak in a field to the left – the Guards in
our rere on the right. The morning was cloudy with a sharp
hoar-frost.

About seven o'clock [*it was about 7.25*] the cry was 'Fall in!' We
ran to the river side and dashed into it, up to our arm-pits in water,
through a shower of musketry from the french. On reaching the opposite shore, my Company and the 2nd ran to cover the riflemen [*the
1st and 2nd Light Battalions K.G.L., who had led the assault*]. But to
make it more clear, I'll endeavour to sketch the attack [Plate 1, *facing
p. 4*].

The Bidassoa is very rapid at the place where I crossed (No. 1)

3

and so very strong was the current that we were constrained to take each other by the arm, holding our swords and muskets in the air, the water being up to the arm pits and knee deep in mud. The French were stationed in the houses opposite, behind the hedges and in the ditches keeping up a regular fire upon us as we struggled through the cold river. Many fell wounded and were drowned through the rapidity of the element. The balls splashed around us like a shower of rain. But the water was so excessively cold and strong that I was insensible to the splashing of the musketry around my chest and I struggled through mechanically, without even reflecting that I was walking to fight a few thousand devils before breakfast.

On reaching the opposite shore we cleared the houses of the French and recovered breath for a few minutes. My company and the 1st under Major Gerber[1] then sallied out. We dived into a wood on the slope of a hill behind every tree of which stood a frenchman, distraction in his eye and death in his hand, popping from the ditches, between the thickets, and among the bushes.

And now I first heard that hissing and plaintive whistling from the balls around me. The hiss is caused by the wind but when [a ball passes] close to you a strong shrill whistle tells you of your escape. I felt no tremor or cold sensation whatever. I walked without thought or reflection.

We soon gained the outside of the wood, the French scampering like rabbits in a warren. On ascending [higher up the hill] a 9 lb. shot from [our own] artillery [across the river] fell short and nearly cut off half of us. We jumped down a ditch to escape its range and, creeping along a hedge, we gained a field which we had to cross to take a small farmhouse (No. 2).

On the edge of the field we became exposed to an elevated battery (No. 3). A heavy shot fell two yards to my left and covered me with mud and slime. The noise was so great and the splash into the earth so violent that I mechanically jumped against a tall Polack who, good-naturedly smiling, pushed me back saying, 'Don't flinch, Ensign.' Little hump-backed Bacmeister[2] behind me also said 'Vall, Veatley, how you like dat?'

'Not good for the kidneys,' I said.

1. Major Arnold Gerber, a talented officer soon to be promoted lieutenant-colonel. He had commanded the detachment of volunteers from the K.G.L. Brigades during the final assault on San Sebastian.

2. Captain Lucas Bacmeister. He had recently returned to the Battalion, having been severely wounded three months previously at Tolosa.

Plate 1 The Scene of the Bidassoa Crossing 7 October 1813.

KEY : 1, *The burned bridge at Béhobie where Wheatley's company crossed under fire from*, 3, *the French battery at Croix des Bouquets, and from*, 4, *the French battery on the Montagne de Louis XIV.* 2, *The Farmhouse which Wheatley's company and Major Gerber's company captured before moving on to take the battery at*, 3.

Plate 2 'Cooking, smoking, eating and drinking form their only amusements.'

That very moment another volley came and cut a fellow to pieces before my face.

I looked up at the battery and fancied every mouth pointed at me alone, and I moved on expecting my two legs off every moment. The idea of flight never entered my mind but the hotter the fire the stronger I felt myself urged to advance. And in spite of the cannon shot, we gained the farmhouse with the loss of one killed and two wounded.

We remained in this house until that accursed battery (No. 3) destroyed it about our ears, and after some consultation we resolved to rush up and endeavour to storm it. This was the hottest part of the action for it was literally rushing into the cannon's mouth. The balls dashed the earth into my eyes. The wind of the shot was sensibly felt. But we panted up the hill, jumped into the ditch, climbed the mud walls. Away ran the French, and thus fell the battery into our hands containing the 10 pounders, plenty of onions, rotten biscuit and hay.

Thank God for this escape, for my pantaloons were simply torn at the right knee, and the flesh blackened by the wind of the ball.

I cannot refrain noticing one circumstance which occurred during this my first battle. While standing in a ditch with my men, popping through the hedges at the enemy as they ran from field to field, the fellow who stood on my left set up a most lamentable roar and, on turning, I found his cheek swelled up like a currant pudding from a ball which, passing downwards, had shattered his jaw and had lodged in his throat. I, like a novice, took out my handkerchief and endeavoured to staunch the blood. But my bullying Captain Nötting bellowed out, 'Wheatley! Mind your duty and leave the man alone!'

Experience afterwards convinced me how unwise was the action, but the sudden impulse of human feeling in the breast of a young soldier was the only answer I could return to the jokes and merriment afterwards practiced upon me.

Colonel Ompteda[1] with the rest of the regiment stormed the other battery (No. 4) at the same time; and the army on our right and left were equally successful excepting the 95th Regiment which did not

1. Lieutenant-Colonel Christian, Baron von Ompteda had recently taken over command of the 5th Line Battalion from Lieutenant-Colonel Baron Bussche, who had been transferred to the command of the 1st Light Battalion. Ompteda, at this time 47 years old, was an excellent officer described by the historian of the King's German Legion as 'a fine soldier who never shrank from danger or difficulties, an officer as distinguished for personal courage, as for all the higher qualities of a soldier and a man'. – Beamish, op. cit, ii, 226, 371. A rather dull book about him, based mainly on his letters to his brother, was compiled by his nephew, Baron Louis von Ompteda. It was translated by John Hill in 1892 and given the English title of *A Hanoverian-English Officer, A Hundred Years Ago.*

succeed until the whole day's fighting enabled them to gain their point.[1]

Thus we entered the French Empire, October the 7th, 1813, about seven o'clock in the morning; and after fighting until four in the afternoon we encamped on the hills (No. 5) where I now write this.

Must not forget to write to Henry to-morrow. I've just returned from burying the dead. How it rains! Poor fellows! No more colds for them.

[*The dead in Wheatley's brigade were nearly all from the 1st and 2nd Light Battalions that led the assault, most of them in the 1st Battalion. The 5th Line Battalion losses, as Wheatley says, were very slight.*

The casualties in the army as a whole were, in fact, very few, considering the number of troops involved, the difficulties of the ground which they had to cross, and the strength of the French defences.

The operation was highly successful and the limited objectives which Wellington had set himself were all achieved. The French army had retreated to the Nivelle, where they began to construct new fortifications, while the Allies had fought their way up the dominating heights from which their enemies had been driven.

The 1st Division looked down upon St Jean de Luz in front of which the French had entrenched themselves in a series of redoubts guarding the port and the river's mouth. Wheatley's battalion faced Urrugne, a small village strongly defended with earthworks and barricades and covered by a battery of heavy guns on the hills of Urtubia behind it.]

12 October The rains are so very violent just now that the dead bodies from the battle last week have swelled and protruded from the earth. One fellow's hand is now out at the back of my tent and from the button I see he is of the 9th Regiment.[2]

---

1. The 95th Regiment became the Rifle Brigade in 1815 when its number was re-allotted to an ordinary line battalion which had the county affiliation of Derbyshire and which later became the 2nd Battalion the Sherwood Foresters. At this time its 1st, 2nd and 3rd Battalions were in the Light Division, which had a far harder battle against Soult's centre than the 1st and 5th Divisions had had against his left. The 2nd Battalion had a particularly bad time and lost more men than all the other battalions involved. – Oman, *op. cit.*, vii, 534.

2. East Norfolk Regiment. It became the Royal Norfolk Regiment in 1881 and now on amalgamation with the Suffolk Regiment has become the 1st East Anglian Regiment. At this time it was in Colonel the Hon. C. J. Greville's Brigade in the 5th Division. It had led the Division's attack at the Bidassoa, and, having crossed the river, had swung to the right over the heights. Hence the grave of one of its men being so near Wheatley's tent.

Wrote to Henry yesterday. Sent him a couple of blades of grass from my tent – conquered spoils!

13 October Last night my turn for outlying piquet opposite the village of Urrugne, on a hill on the left. Cold wet and windy, without tents or covering. The French fires very numerous behind the village. I smoke a great deal when out all night as I think it prevents cold, spends the time and encourages meditation. Very wet.

25 October Respecting the Germans among whom I have now lived a twelvemonth, I can only judge sparingly, for to presume giving an opinion on an entire nation from an experience gained by a few months' intercourse with a company of soldiers, would be judging by supposition and rendering doubtful every assertion connected with national peculiarities or original characteristics. What respectability I have found among my brother soldiers, when supported by a good education and urbanity of manners, I cannot distinguish from that always natural to a British Gentleman and which renders society so pleasing and acquaintance so valuable. The Generality of Officers in the Legion are affable, friendly and pleasing; but their manner of address [is sometimes haughty and reserved].

The German soldiers employ the whole of their leisure hours over the fire. Cooking, smoking, eating and drinking form their only amusements, and so incessantly and unceasingly do they indulge themselves in these peculiarities that they become heavy-eyed, sallow and dull in every action of sense and body.

I'll just step out and seize a group. I shan't want for models[1] [Plate 2, *facing p. 5*].

26 October This night on piquet covering the light troops, and a most severe and rigidly cold night it was. About 2 a.m. the

1. Pipe smoking in Wellington's army was not at all common at this time outside the King's German Legion. But the Germans, both the soldiers and their wives, seem constantly to have been puffing at their pipes, as Wheatley suggests. Wheatley himself preferred cigars, which Captain John Kincaid of the 95th thought an essential part of the contents of every officer's haversack. A 'well regulated one ought never to be without the following furniture,' Kincaid wrote, 'a couple of biscuit, a sausage, a little tea and sugar, a knife, fork and spoon, a tin cup, a pair of socks, a piece of soap, a tooth brush, towel and comb, and half a dozen cigars'. – Captain J. Kincaid, *Adventures in the Rifle Brigade* (1829), 33–34.

Cacadores[1] on our right and the French outposts opposite exchanged half a dozen shots. We also took an Hanoverian and his wife in the act of desertion. They were concealed in a bush. Seven deserters came over to us this night. One had a black eye from his Officer.

27 October The French appear buisy in fortifying themselves about a mile in our front. A fine clear day.

28 October Most winterly and stormy. The Pyrenees around us are covered with snow, presenting a most romantic but cheerless scene. The rain pours down in torrents and two blankets over my tent are insufficient to prevent the ingress of the elements. My paper is damp, my fingers cold, my heart cheerless.

29 October Five brigades of artillery have been sent off to the right and daily expectations of a tough battle are very prevalent.

The Germans bear excessive fatigues wonderfully well, and a German will march over six leagues [*about eighteen miles*] while an Englishman pants and perspires beneath the labour of twelve miles; but before the enemy a German moves on silent but mechanically, whilst an Englishman is all sarcasm, laughter and indifference.

The Germans are the only nation who can reside with the English without giving rise to those national prejudices so common when two nations for a time abide together. The German Legion is a compound of Saxons, Poles, Swedes, Hungarians, Prussians, Russians, French and Dutch. There is scarce a soldier but speaks two or three languages

1. Although they were officially known as *caçadores* these Portuguese light infantry battalions, as, indeed, the light battalions of the K.G.L. were not all armed with rifles, of which there were no more than 4,000 in the entire army. Most men had muskets, as all men had in the line battalions. These muskets were 'East India' pattern, a modification of the 'Brown Bess' which had been in use for a century or so. They had a smooth bore and were muzzle-loaded and could not be fired accurately, even by the most expert shot, at ranges above eighty yards.

The rifle was accurate up to 300 yards, but it was just as liable to misfire as the musket and was even more difficult to load, as the charge had to be rammed down a rifled barrel. Few riflemen could load and fire – which they had to do standing up – in much less than thirty seconds, about twice as long as the time it took to load and fire a musket.

The tactics of Wellington's army – the lines of men standing almost shoulder to shoulder to fire and forming squares or oblongs with fixed bayonets which could not be outflanked by cavalry – were, of course, dictated by the unreliability, the inaccuracy and the slow reloading processes of small arms.

Much of the muddle of the battles, too, was caused by the musket which (since smokeless powder was not introduced until the 1880s) filled the field with clouds of white, obscuring smoke.

and their practice of desertion is so prevalent that they learn by rote and speak foreign languages in spite of themselves.

The German soldiery do not respect much their officers because they remember many of their comrades on sentry and have frequently beaten the Sentinels' Tattoo[1] with them. The officers, besides, do not hesitate to accompany a reproof with a blow and I cannot imagine any man so dejected in situation as to bear patiently corporal chastisement. I could not strike a fellow soldier who notwithstanding a musket of thirteen lbs. weight, a knapsack with his whole wardrobe on his back (as well as his belly ammunition and sixty rounds of ball cartridges) will cheerfully carry your sword for you. And I've seen a lazy officer or two not blush in asking him. It is really astonishing how the human form can support all that weight. The pressure of the straps on the collar bones and chest I should think enough to weary the poor fellows even in a stationary duty, let alone in forty miles of marching.

Five sentries of the 1st [*Light Battalion K.G.L.*] fired off their pieces just now as a signal and ran over to the enemy. One of my company, one of the 2nd Line and one of the Foot Guards went over this morning, thus eight ran over to their country's foes. Two Frenchmen just came over.

Lord Wellington four miles to our right.[2]

Weather unfavourable and harassing. Winter fast approaching.

On piquet every other night we make large fires and contrive to stupify ourselves with brandy and tobacco. We now live on biscuit and salt beef.

31 October   Four Germans deserted an hour ago. Its a matter of astonishment what can induce these men to run over to the French, above all when so many months' pay is due to them. The only reason I can suppose for the frequency of the practice is the inclemency of the season, the harassing duty just now, and the badness of our tents.

Perhaps these traitors imagine that should they reach the French outposts they will be instantly forwarded to some depot where [they will be] fed without labour and sheltered from the merciless weather.

1. This phrase appears to have had no special significance. Captain Cyril Falls has written to the editor to say, 'I too have never heard this phrase. Did they just borrow a drum and join the drummer, perhaps when well warmed with wine? I need not say their reputation was fine.' Mr Eric Partridge endorses this view: 'After careful consideration I'm forced to conclude that Cyril Falls is right.... I don't know of any military slang expression justifying us reading something more into it than this.'

2. Wellington had moved his headquarters up from Lesaca to Vera on 10 October.

1 November   Most dreadful squalls in the Bay of Biscay. Hail, snow, rain and wind, thunder and lightning. Firing in our rere. Artillery and musketry for hours. Can form no conjecture. Dreadful night. The straw I sleep on is wet and a drizzly rain comes through my tent. Chilly and damp.

2 November   Intelligence reached us this morning that Pamplona had surrendered with 4,000 men and four Generals.[1] Two transports full of our troops lost in the Bay. A brig stranded last night. Good news from Germany.[2] Fine morning. It appears evident, as far as my spare knowledge of politics will allow me to presume, that the summer of the French Emperor's military career has nearly closed and that his Autumn is shedding its last leaves.

Who can tell but I may once more see my native land and be very happy. Yet appearances are bad just now and I dare not commit to paper certain occurrencies which destroy every pleasing reflection and would be grinned at by some callous booby.

Should my destruction be necessary in this arduous task in which I'm now associated, well, I forgive all my enemies at home and may the cause of my melancholy moments be happier than I. I [do wish] her so. But it's time for my piquet. I perceive the men are falling in.

3 November   On piquet last night on the high road. A cold night. Smoked the whole time. Really, a soldier's life is not so idle neither, for I've not had a night's rest this last week! But am in good health. Wonder what Henry is doing.

There is no difference between this and the other side of the Bidassoa. I've seen one or two countrymen here, and their dress is the same as the Spaniards' – a large slouched hat; the jacket in cold or hot, wet or dry weather is thrown over the left shoulder; the right hand always grasps a huge cudgel; the waistcoat long and of blue velvet; the breeches loose at the knees and without being braced up; a red sash round the waist; and stockings rolled round the top of the calf completes the national dress of the *paysans* of Biscay.

The women work more than the men and are remarkable for a

1. Pamplona surrendered on 31 October to the Spanish General, Don Carlos de España. Wellington was anxiously waiting for news of this, as he intended to give orders for the continuation of his attack as soon as it was confirmed. The garrison numbered 3,800 combatants under General Louis Pierre Cassan.

2. The Battle of Leipzig had ended on 19 October with the desertion of Napoleon's last German allies and the rout of his army.

simularity of feature through the whole province indiscriminately. They are brunettes of rather pretty, thin physiognomy, being what is termed 'interesting'. There is a national peculiarity in their manner of dressing for their hair is drawn back very tight from the forehead to the back of the head, and being twisted is suffered to hang down the back as low as the shoulder blade, and the longer the handsomer. The colour is jet black. The neck is bare, the bosom never so but covered with a red handkerchief like our servant girls in the country. Their stays are very stiff and high and the waist is so contracted that they appear to have uncommon large hips and make an appearance as peculiar as antique. Few wear shoes or stockings or even bonnets, be the weather ever so inclement. I'll endeavour to sketch one of each [Plate 3, *facing p.* 12].

4 November Two soldiers this morning were punished notwithstanding the severity of the weather. They severally received eight hundred lashes for attempting to desert.[1] In spite of several arguments held out by Sir F. Burdet[2] for the abolition of corporal chastisement, I am confident no other substitute could effectually check and restrain so many thousands of men from the commission of those crimes to be expected from such an heterogeneous mixture of depravity and ignorance as is to be met with in an army. Imprisonment would encourage the dilatory; stoppages of pay would increase the dishonest; reproofs are useless; disgraces would soon become common; transportation must thin the ranks; and death become dangerous when too commonly inflicted. The only safe, the only effective remedy is Castigation. And as the noble Baron [*Baronet*] is not or ever was a military character, his opinion is merely supposition erected on a foundation of charity and humanity for his fellow creatures which undoubtedly is a dangerous one when [applied] to all. A public and national speculation

1. They presumably did not receive these eight hundred lashes all at once. A surgeon was always present at floggings to decide when a man's life was in danger. At the surgeon's orders the man was cut down, and when he had sufficiently recovered was taken back to the triangle made of sergeants' halberds for the continuation of the punishment. Few men could survive more than two hundred lashes at one time. The maximum punishment was twelve hundred lashes; but this was rarely awarded. Sentences of a thousand lashes were awarded more than fifty times, however, during the course of the war. Many men were killed by such treatment. – C. W. C. Oman, *Wellington's Army 1809–1814* (1912), 237–54.

2. Sir Francis Burdett (1770–1844), the great reformer and advocate of popular rights. A passionate opponent of corporal punishment in the Army, he spoke repeatedly against it in the House of Commons as Member for the City of Westminster. He married Sophia, daughter of Thomas Coutts, the banker, in 1793, and succeeded his grandfather as fifth baronet in 1797. Most officers in the Army, like Wheatley, did not share his views.

should never be canvassed in an individual light but comprehensively analysed, not looked upon with the eye of a father of a family but maturely considered with the discernment of a ruler of a nation.

Strong reports of a speedy advance. This day five years where shall I be? *Pro patria mori!*

5 November Fine cold day. The whole of the hill on which we have been encamped since our entry into the French territories was once covered with thick furze, high and strong grass. But now the incessant heavy rains have so softened the soil that the footsteps of men and beasts have completely eradicated every vestige of provender or weed, and the whole mountain bears an appearance of having been ploughed up.

Saw the French Army through a good glass. They were drawn up in line and look clean and well as far as I can discern. Poor tools of affluent ambitious men! Mere machines of politicians! Another month and many of you will lay low and still for ever. The French people are our common enemy, yet I like them as a nation and I really am of opinion every Englishman does the same in his heart.

7 November We've had one or two frosty days which circumstance has dried up the immense quantity of mud and filth everywhere prevalent; and as we wait only for the bye roads to become passable for artillery we look forward anxiously for the day to advance. But this morning presented us with an uncomfortable, rainy, thick, damp, cheerless day. [All the same,] that we engage before three days is a supposition of the greatest probability. The enemy's lines, as they appear through the glass, seem strongly fortified with mud batteries and breastworks, so the greatest likelihood exists of the battle being a most sanguinary one.

All soldiers are predesinarians and if 'tis pre-ordained I should fall I'll die with credit I hope – suppose I write to Henry and Miss B[rookes], Llewellyn[1] and myself have made our wills to each other, and he certainly will do me the last office of sending them.

8 November Just returned from piquet. Fine cold night it was. Llewellyn and I yesterday like two schoolboys passed the sentries at

---

1. Lieutenant Henry Llewellyn of the 5th Battalion appears to have been Wheatley's closest friend. They sailed for Spain in the same ship and joined the battalion on the same day. Wheatley's portrait of him is *facing p. 44*.

Plate 3 'There is a national peculiarity in their manner of dressing.'

Plate 4 The Road leading up to Urrugne.

the hazard of being shot, and running into a small house found some fine grapes. Hearing a groan I went into the loft and found a poor peasant stinking and almost putrid from a musket shot received by chance in the engagement last month. Llewellyn ran back to the camp and brought little Gerson[1] but the case is desparate – he'll die.

7 O'clock. Rumours in the Camp. 'What?' says Schuck,[2] 'I'll run and see.'

An order to stand under arms at three to-morrow – a battle for certain. Must pack up. The last time perhaps. Schuck has promised to send my two letters in case of death. Farewell to all! God help me!!

9 November Been under arms since three o'clock. That infernal Brigade Major[3] mistook the order.

I could not help observing this morning as we stood round the fires how pallid and deathy every countenance appeared. Perhaps my own state of mind exaggerated every appearance as there is something very awful in reflecting that another hour and we may be summoned to that 'bourne from whence no traveller returns'.

Tis a fine frosty morning but the sun smiles sickly upon me. Turned my old servant Bob off just now for impertinence and disrespect. He now shall face that bully death when fool [that he is] he might have remained tranquil with the baggage. We know not what's to our benefit. One moment's indescretion is oft productive of severe regret. To-morrow we again stand under arms and the baggage being ordered to Irun is a certainty of approaching havock. What is Henry doing? *Adieu!*

10 November Packed up at three o'clock a.m. and sent all the baggage to Irun with the tents. Stood round the fires expecting every moment the awful word. The morning was a clear, starlit, frosty one. The different groups around several fires, together with the distant lights of the enemy, had a most superb appearance. A distant approaching, clashing and murmur announced the signal. Nothing was heard but the unhooking of muskets. The fires stood deserted, excepting a solitary drummer boy shivering with apprehension and cold, or a soldier kneeling to the fire, lighting perhaps his last pipe.

1. Dr G. H. Gerson, the battalion's Assistant Surgeon.
2. Ensign Lewis Schuck, the battalion's Adjutant. He was killed at Waterloo.
3. Major Frederick, Baron von Dreschel. Despite this mistake, he was in the opinion of Major Beamish, 'a young officer of high acquirements and great promise'. He was killed in April 1814 at Bayonne.

We now silently groped down the hill, crossed the high road and, breaking through a hedge, skulked along the ditches, no one daring to speak according to orders. The men were ordered to carry their muskets horizontally to prevent the gleaming of the bayonets from betraying our approach. Some fires being on our left, we crawled slowly and silently taking a circuit to the right, when suddenly whirling in a circular manner to the left, we pounced upon the dozing french piquet at the fire and seized them all without a shot's expense. In the same crafty manner we crept along the bye paths, and through the hedges with a country guide until we arrived under some trees where we halted and drew up in a close column. We were then ordered to lay down quietly without speaking a word. Waiting for day-break the cold was so excessive that sleep overpowered me. Judge of my surprise on being awoke at twilight to find myself before the French, who were in position immediately in our front.

[*The 5th Division were still, as at the Bidassoa crossing, on the extreme left of the line, with the 1st Division, supported as before by Lord Aylmer's independent brigade, on their right. The left wing of the army, which included also Portuguese and Spanish troops, was now commanded by Lieutenant-General Sir John Hope, as Sir Thomas Graham had had to go home because his eyes were troubling him again. The 1st Division was still commanded by Major-General Kenneth Howard; but there were certain alterations in its grouping. The second Guards brigade (the 1st and 3rd Battalions of the 1st Foot Guards and a company of the 60th Rifles[1] commanded by Colonel Peregrine Maitland) had now arrived from Oporto, and the battalions of the K.G.L. had been split into two brigades, the two light battalions (known, because of the colour of their uniforms, as 'Halkett's Green Germans') remaining under Colonel Halkett, but the three line battalions passing under command of Major-General Heinrich von Hinüber.[2]*

The part which the left wing were to play in the forthcoming attack — although Wheatley seems never to have been aware of the fact — was purely a diversionary one.

Wellington's plan was to put in his attack farther up the Nivelle, as

1. Both these riflemen and those in the other Guards brigade were from the 5th Battalion of the 60th. Most of them were Germans 'whose record in the war stands comparison with any in the army'. – Michael Glover, *Wellington's Peninsular Victories* (Batsford, 1963), 23.

2. For the complete order of battle of the army at this time see Appendix A of *Wellington: The Bidassoa and the Nivelle*, by Major-General F. C. Beatson (1931).

Soult had expected he would at the Bidassoa, and then advance towards the sea to outflank the St Jean de Luz position, while the left wing were to make a formidable pretence of attacking this position from the front. It is this energetic feint which Wheatley describes.]

A cannon ball whizzing over us gave us notice of our situation. So jumping up, we took our positions and stood exposed the whole morning to the incessant bombardment of the batteries [*on the hill behind Urrugne*]. A dreadful firing was heard on our right and the light companies of our several battalions kept up a sharp skirmishing in the woods at the bottom of the hills on which the enemy's artillery and infantry were both strongly fortified. In the meantime the 84th Regiment[1] on the high road endeavoured to storm the village of Urrugne. But the French had so stopped up the entrance with piles [of] cartwheels and old lumber that a miserable havock ensued from the cross firing from the windows and roofs of the houses [on each side]. The following is a correct sketch of the entrance as I took it one fine morning on piquet with Llewellyn [Plate 4, *facing p.* 13].

About two o'clock a brigade of light artillery tore into the field where we stood and beating down some houses on the right of the village, the 84th once more made into Urrugne and breaking down the fences seized the front houses and took the village house by house.[2]

About three o'clock the firing became very hot and as the number of wounded increased, it was decided to send a strong reinforcement forward into the wood to the right of Urrugne. As usual, my spiteful commander, Nötting, sent me in first with six men and Sergeant Hüler.

On running from tree to tree I met my friend Boyd[3] chewing some grapes and we stood for some time eating together. Then we agreed to enter a house at a little distance and annoy the French from the windows. So collecting our men with his bugle, we ran forward and entering it, fastened the door with some timber and old tubs. Leaving two men to defend it we went upstairs and found the top composed of one room full of straw, chestnut peel and old rags.

1. The York and Lancaster Regiment. This was its 2nd Battalion, which, with the 76th and 85th Foot, was in Aylmer's brigade. It was on Wheatley's right.

2. According to Napier this service was performed by the 85th Regiment not the 84th. – Major-General Sir W. F. P. Napier, *History of the War in the Peninsula and in the South of France* revised edition, 1882, v, 376.

3. Lieutenant George Boyd of the 1st Line Battalion K.G.L. He had been wounded in June at Tolosa.

We called and collected our men [and they fired out of the windows and] struck every frenchman they saw.

As we were sheltered from the batteries over against us by the trees, we might have defended the house until night. But a strong body of about thirty french with an officer at their head were seen running to our little castle and the two rascals at the door downstairs [deserted their post and] came rushing up pale and aghast and bursting open our door communicated their panick to the rest. All that Boyd and myself could do to stop the fools was ineffectual. They plunged headlong out of [a] window at the bottom of which ran a small rivulet. Boyd then hearing the french coming up cried out, 'It's no use, Wheatley, follow me!' We both leapt out the very instant the door burst open. I fell most violently on my right arm. Boyd sprang up from his hands and knees and making for a tree before him received a volley from the window and a ball entering his head passed out between the eyes. He fell dead. As good an open hearted lad as ever breathed. Many a segar have we smoked together, and many a tedious night have we braved the elements together.

For my part I gained a tuft of trees without any accident except my boot torn at the ankle and the flesh lacerated; but at the time the blow appeared as if I had struck my foot against a stone and 'twas only next morning I discovered the mistake.

I retreated from tree to tree, not knowing where to go, but meeting young Pascal[1] he told me my Regiment was relieved by the 2nd Battalion. So leaving the forest I regained my Battalion, which I found in the same place.

Lying down opposed only to the cannon shot of the foe, Colonel Ompteda, Llewellyn, his two nephews[2] and self sat down on the grass, chatting and watching the fight for three or four hours; and although I did not relish the cannon balls now and then tearing the earth about us, I saw no change in the colonel's countenance and he laughed and joked his little nephew for holding his breath as they flew over us like a passing whirlwind. The battle was uncommonly noisy on our right.

As soon as night came the Adjutant sent word twas my turn for Battalion Guard at the entrance of the wood.

Hungry, tired and wet, I took my stand. But the cold was so violent that I opened the sergeant's knapsack about twelve o'clock and, telling

1. Lieutenant George Frederick Pascal, 2nd Line Battalion K.G.L.
2. Ensign Christian Ludwig, Baron Ompteda and Louis, Baron Ompteda, both of the 6th Line Battalion K.G.L. Christian was 16 and Louis only 14. Their uncle described them in a letter home as very good, willing boys but far too young to be at war.

Plate 5a 'My little castle – a stable in a miserable barn near Fuenterrabia.'

Plate 5b 'The House [at Ahetze] is situated in a thick wood.'

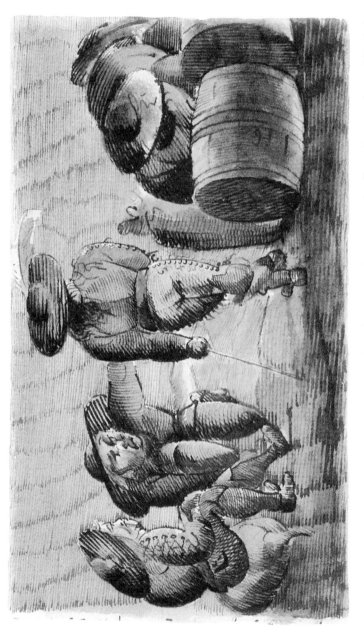

Plate 6 'The more buttons they can sow on their waistcoats and trowsers, the finer they are dressed in their own opinion.'

the sentry to wake me if he heard a footstep, I rolled myself in the Sergeant's blanket and slept at the foot of a tree.

A violent kick in the neck awoke me suddenly and the Colonel's voice of 'What's this white thing?' soon brought me on my legs. A most severe reprimand and threat ensued for sleeping before the enemy, and I was constrained to walk up and down for some hours.

On the Colonel's repeating his round he kindly apologised for kicking me, and on my telling him all was still and that the fires on the French batteries bore a suspicious aspect, he agreed with me and walked for an hour with me. I then leaned against a tree and dozed until daybreak.

A sudden order to bring up the guard roused me and on joining the Regiment I found the whole Brigade under arms and entering into the wood. Each battalion took a different [route] and setting off [after the 5th] I found we were running up the hill behind Urrugne to take the battery at [the] top.

When three parts up I suddenly sank into the earth and when I recovered myself I found myself on the trunk of a fallen tree, surrounded by an Officer of the Artillery, two or three men and a surgeon dressing a large gash on my right thigh. My foot was bound tight between two pieces of flat wood and on asking what was the matter, the Officer told me he had taken me out of a deep mine with two others, that my ankle was seriously disjointed and a spike from the bottom had entered my thigh. My Servant, Shernavissenar, just then returned with some water, and the Artillery Officer kindly ordered his men to make me a flat bed with some sticks and I was thus carried to the Major's house in Urrugne. On being carried up the steps a tall German Cavalry Officer stuck his huge mustachios into my face and asked me if he could assist me in any way, which kind offer I refused, and on being placed in the parlor I sent Shernavissenar for my [mule which I call] Eliza from Irun.

On her arrival I managed to sit on her and my servant leading, I rode about three hours. The rain then fell in torrents and what with wet and pain and overtaking the wounded limping and groaning [it was] not the pleasantest morning I have spent in my life. About half a mile from the burnt bridge [across the Bidassoa] looking from under my boat cloak[1] at a little house on the left, I saw a man standing

---

1. The heavy cape of naval origin often worn by officers either over or instead of a greatcoat. It could be carried rolled on the saddle and was better for sleeping in than a greatcoat.

in a cocked hat with a long feather. Methought I recognised my old schoolfellow Beverley;[1] and the following confab ensued:

'Do I see Beverley?'

'You do, sir.'

'Don't you know me?'

'No, sir.'

'Look again.'

'I think I recall your features, yet you have the advantage of me.'

'I *formerly* had the advantage of *you* at Hammersmith when I fought you with pistols at the end of Lotherington's garden.'

'Good God! Is your name Wheatley? How came you in the Army? How pale you look. Come in. What's the matter?' &c, &c.

I foolishly alighted, threw a buttock of cold beef into a consumption, and gave so violent an emitic to a couple of bottles of wine that all the day's disaster was forgotten, and I reached the hospital about midnight in which I awoke the next morning in a furious fever which nearly finished my campaigning.

Here I now am lying in a stable in a miserable barn near Fuenterrabia. The family consists of one peasant about forty, two elderly, half-starved women (his wife and her sister) and an Irishwoman of an English regiment who lives here because she cannot live anywhere else. Her room is in a loft to which she ascends by a ladder. Under the slope stands a solitary ass with a bell under its jaw in continual motion to prevent its being stolen. My bed is in some straw laid over with a blanket. My trunk is my pillow and my boat cloak my counterpane. At my feet stand my horse which I call Sam and my mule, Eliza. When they have eaten their hay the latter pricks up her ears and seems to smile at me for more.

I'm now scrawling this on my right side on the moist floor. My servant is gone to Irun for meat and hay and I am downright wretched.

Wrote to Henry and Headreach[2] this morning. Enclosed a couple of assignats[3] found in the Mayor's house.

13 November   Beverley just visited me. Lent me twenty-five dollars.[4]

1. Charles W. Beverley, Deputy Assistant Commissary-General. Being staff officers, as the term was then used, commissaries were entitled to wear the cocked hat and feathers of staff uniform.

2. This name is scarcely decipherable and neither the editor nor Wheatley's descendants know who he was.

3. French paper money in use 1789–97.

4. A Spanish dollar was worth about five shillings at this time.

Read my intended posthumous letters and memorandums to him. Offered to buy my favourite horse. Refused. The Spanish horses are long in the leg and neck and back. They possess not the strength of our Cavalry horses, only making a shew on parade. Their tails are uncropped and tis remarkable that all horses in the Peninsula are marked with a hot iron on the broad part of the thigh or neck. The Portuguese mark is distinguished from the Spanish. A colt is as regularly marked as an infant is baptised.

15 November Carmichael[1] from over the way drank tea with me last night and read Burns's poems to me until eleven o'clock.[2]

About twelve, just as my wounds were dressed and I had fallen asleep, my landlord with his lamp awoke me by saying several men were outside the door demanding admittance. I ordered my servant who lay snoring near my animals to tell them the house was an English hospital and that half a mile further was the village of Oyarzun. I could hear a confused noise and a heavy rain falling on the roof above me. All remonstrance was vain and they broke in very quickly to the number of thirty-five with a drum and a color, and, filling the room in which the poor people slept, soon kindled a large fire and called for wine and tobacco.

Unknowing how to act and knowing the ferocity of these Spanish rascals, I advised my servant to load his musket and give it me and then to run to Oyarzun half a mile off and tell Dr Kohrs[3] I wanted a couple of Grenadiers from the hospital Guard. By all that's sacred the coward was afraid to go alone, pretending he would not leave me to be murdered! So ordering him to tell the landlord slyly to come to me without being noticed, I desired him to do as I had ordered Sherna-vissenar, and when he returned to knock gently three times at the stable door when I would let them in. My servant let him out and joining the rabble in the next room, pretended to drink and entertain them. Meantime I put my pantaloons on with the utmost pain and taking out my sabre, hid it under the straw to my left. My dollars I put underneath my blanket on which I lay and then, covering up, waited with the utmost trepidation for the expected signal.

The noisy hilarity and laughing in the next room increased the

1. Lieutenant Alexander Carmichael, 1st Line Battalion K.G.L.
2. Robert Burns had died in 1796, but most of his work was published posthumously and some had only recently appeared.
3. Dr Kohrs, Assistant Surgeon, 5th Line Battalion K.G.L.

melancholy of my dark abode and I heard at intervals the broken Spanish of the Irish woman whose bad disposition and depravity of principle I more dreaded than the whole *banditti* then with her.

I suddenly heard something groping about. My heart palpitated and presently I felt a hand on my shoulder pass over my breast and feel my knees. Then the noise retreated. I unhooked my servant's bayonet and held it under the clothes, expecting a return. How I dreaded the wished for signal should these wretches be in my place of rest!

Suddenly three soldiers entered without arms. One held a lighted piece of wood from the fire which he had brought to my face. I closed my eyes pretending to sleep, while the two opened my other trunk placed at my feet to keep them warm; in this trunk I keep my tea, sugar, biscuit and dirty linen. They completely emptied it. About five minutes after they had returned to their comrades I thought I heard a knock. Seizing my sword I jumped to the door and listening, heard the three knocks. Lifting away gently the log of wood which closed it, I whispered, 'Who's there?' And the landlord cried '*Ci, signor.*'

I ordered the two soldiers with him to rush into the room where the Spanish were and to huzza very loud, but not to fire a shot and by no means to kill anyone.

I rushed in as well as I could, followed by the two soldiers, and upset two or three clean into the fire. One man who fell on his side in the flame fortunately set his cartridge box on fire which, exploding, filled the room with smoke. The Irishwoman screamed out 'Oh! Ensign! have mercy!' Shernavissenar jumped on one young fellow and knocked about him like a madman. And all would have succeeded without accident had not my irritable temper got the better of my reason, and seeing the door choked up in the eagerness to escape on the part of the Spaniards, I seized a man by the Collar to drag him back. He turned round and with his firelock struck me [so] violently on my sword arm that I nearly fell to the ground. With a cut between a thrust and a slash, I opened his cheek. At the same instant one of the men behind me thrust his bayonet over my shoulder through the knapsack and into the back of a spaniard. My head was beginning to swim round. My servant carried me to my bed and the poor peasant gratefully brought me some wine and chestnuts. Then ordering the doors to be well fastened and each soldier to stand Sentry two hours alternately I slept sound till eleven this morning.

Carmichael just left me about four o'clock. Two or three hours ago I was again annoyed by some spaniards. But on getting up I found a gruff-looking fellow with two muskets on his shoulder at the door and two behind him. My blood was up instantly and I sent the [fellow] reeling back; and it being slimy he fell to the ground with a rattle of muskets. Hearing a fellow behind cry out *'Caracho!'* (a word used by the Spanish when influenced by any passion) I seized one to attack him, but I fell from my weak foot.

I cannot help recalling the indifferent behaviour of Carmichael who stood aloof with the entire use of his limbs and I am resolved to read this paragraph to him when he comes to-night. The rain now drips through the tiles over my head.

17 November   Getting better. A painful running from my thigh. The instant I can walk I am resolved to join the Army. I shall be frozen here or else murder'd.

18 November   Beverley called this morning. These Commissaries have an easy life of it. Very wet with sleet.

21 November   Been out for the first time and have sketched my little castle from a bank opposite [Plate 5a, *facing p.* 16].

23 November   Took a ride this morning. Gave my poor landlord a couple of pounds of fresh meat, which he has not tasted for many years, he says. The poor peasants live upon chestnuts and sour wine. People in England know not the distress of a country ravaged by contending armies.

24 November   Eleven o'clock P.M. This morning I rode to Irun and saw two spanish soldiers dying for want of food. One of them lay in the open street – a perfect atomy. And his feeble cry of *'Oh! Officire Inglais'* made me miserable all the way home.

28 November   Ten O'clock. Last evening had almost been my last. The evening being uncommonly serene, Carmichael and self strolled down the high road to visit Henderson.[1] When we reached the bridge half way to Irun and leaned over the place, chatting and viewing the [stream,] some muleteers passed and one of these, mounted on his

1. Ensign John Henderson, Artillery, K.G.L.

mule with a tub of aqua dentae[1] on each side, drove his beast so near that the barrel struck me on the hip and very nearly fetched me over the bridge. On recovering myself, I overtook the fellow whistling unconcernedly along and sent him clean off with a left hander. He ran up cursing me to the Diable with ten thousand *'carachos'*, but I pitched in a stomacher and sent him reeling.

Thinking I had given him enough, I was limping back to Carmichael who suddenly exclaimed 'Take care, Wheatley!' and on turning round saw the fellow aiming his carbine and instantly fire. The ball whizzed by my right side and fell five or six yards before Carmichael who instantly set off after him but he leaped over the ditch and we seized his mule and delivered it to the Commissaries Store.

These muleteers are very numerous and monopolised by the Commissariat. They receive a dollar daily for each beast and their rations extra. They are just now fourteen months in arrears and it is a good pledge for their security.[2]

The greatest part of these rascals carry long knives in their breeches and they do not scruple using them at times. They all sing one air and their themes are extempore. The more buttons a muleteer can sow on his waistcoat and trowsers, the finer he is dressed in his own opinion [Plate 6, *facing p.* 17].

They drink the liquers entrusted to their conveyance and fill up the vacancy with salt water – a nauseous beverage.

They are all liable to deductions of pay for any loss of baggage entrusted to them. They carry carbines and in Winter tis easy to trace the road of a herd of cattle by the carcasses dropping occasionally through fatigue and starvation.

There are thousands of these Muleteers now in the employment of the Commissariat and they are so accustomed to the jogging of the beasts and the beasts are so used to the nodding of their riders that they both sleep and ride and walk together. These carriers intoxicate

1. Aguadiente – the name by which Spanish brandy was then commonly known.
2. 'Our muleteers are now owed twenty-one months' pay', the Judge Advocate-General wrote in his diary in January 1814. 'They have therefore their own way, and are under no control at all. Nothing but a sort of *esprit de corps*, and the fear of losing all claim to the debt, makes them keep with us at all, and we must submit to their fraud and carelessness, and have no remedy.
'As an instance, I may mention that one brigade of mules, who had 24,000 pounds of barley given them to bring here, five leagues from Pasajes, only delivered 18,000 and openly, almost admitted, they had taken the rest which I suppose they had sold to raise money.' – Larpent, *The Private Journal of Judge Advocate F. S. Larpent*, ii, 233.

themselves at times but not to make a common practice of it like my Countrymen. On long Journeys they sleep under hedges and down the ditches. When riding along through quags and bogs, over heaths and through forests pitch dark, I've frequently heard these people discoursing among the brambles and thickets. We are always prepared for action as they carry short carbines [as well as] long knives and are notorious thieves and murderers.

Good breeding is not their characteristic for they always prefer the cleanest part of the road and never turn aside, let the person passing be of ever so respectable an appearance or class. We have many skirmishes with them and I've engaged in many a foolish encounter with them.

The houses, viz. the farm houses, are one and the same in make and shape, completely *multum in parvo* – all roof and no bowels. The greater part have no chimnies but suffer the smoke to ooze through the tiling. Consequently the woodwork resembles the beams of a house partly consumed by fire. The house [where I am now] is the facsimile of those I'm writing of. Every poor family keeps an Ass to fetch wood or fuel and a good thing it is. No tax can deprive them of this luxury.

The whole family huddles together round a fire like the wild Irish. The last [visit] in the day is to their animal and after giving him provender they leave him.

The poor landlord or his sister awake me every two hours to recruit his manger. They know very well when 'tis empty by the silence of a little bell under the donkey's jaw.

Cattle draw the burthens in Biscay. These oxen are small and of a dunn color, much like our Alderneys. The peasants in Biscay exist on indian corn and chesnuts which they mix into a paste excessively heavy to the stomach. They form them into pancakes and toast them on the fire.

The country people have a peculiar method of ploughing up their fields, which is performed by an instrument like a three pronged pitchfork but much longer in the teeth and rather curved at the points. When four of five people of both sexes in a line work together tis strange to perceive the exactitude of their motions and the quantity of soil turned over by this process of agriculture in a short time.

There are a set of infernal-looking beings (inhabitants of the Asturias) who journey far and wide with immense loads of butter [Plate 7, *facing p. 32*]. Their ears and necks are laden with silver images and they are the most repugnant class of human flesh I ever saw.

29 November   A Spanish Officer with three horses begged just now a night's lodging in my room which I refused for I hate a Spaniard more than a Frenchman.

30 November   Twelve o'clock P.M. Been all day at Fuenterrabia with Beverley whom I met at Irun in Church. I heard a band play in the Church during the service. The execution was admirable. The French and Spaniards drum alike and the tune is dum, dum, dum, dum, dummery, dum, dum.

Beverley is to send to-morrow for my Eliza whom I sold to him for thirty dollars, an order being issued from Head-quarters that all Subalterns are to keep but one animal. Have made up my mind to set off the day after to-morrow, Beverley having promised to lend me a mule and muleteer up to my Regiment, but where to find it is the difficulty having heard nothing lately.

1 December   All packed up. Gave my landlord eight dollars which produced a stare of astonishment and a million of benedictions. The Irish woman begged my Charity, but I saw her pour brandy down the throat of her little suckling one morning probably with intent to kill it, so I gave her a little tea and sugar. Have ordered a pot of soup and indian corn to be made, as I intend supping with these poor people tonight. Carmichael coming.

My ankle is still weak and my flesh wound looks blue; but exercise will do wonders. I now must pack up this as I have had time enough to count every tile and pile in this wretched hovel. I shall never forget its infernal Architecture. Amen!

4 December   At six in the morning the day before yesterday Beverley called with a muleteer, a spare mule and one loaded with half a sack of corn and the hind quarter of a bullock for me. My servant Shernavissenar closed the procession with my Samuel laden with his master's baggage.

Just as we were leaving the outward gate of Irun, the Spanish sentry presented his bayonet at my mule's chest and desired me to return. I, of course, out with my sword and desired him to be off. Beverley, who speaks Spanish very well, went to the Officer on Guard who came sputtering and swearing and a frightful scene ensued. He wished me, I suppose (I understood not one word), at the lowest cell of the Inquisition, and I as kindly cursed his Spanish eyes to the bottomless pit.

Meanwhile Beverley gallop'd back to the Corregidor to obtain a pass-port and I stood surrounded and fortified with my beef and baggage, swearing that the first man who touched my bridle should have his head open, and the Officer and Sentry vowing to let the light of heaven into my body if I stirred an inch more forward.

A Spanish officer came up from the Crowd and addressing me in English to my surprise, informed me the order was to let any one in at the gate but to suffer no one to go out. He at the same time advised me to be still, for these Spaniards were very brave when no danger appeared. He said he was from Dublin and hated the rascals heartily, but circumstances compelled him to act so.

Beverley now returned with a passport, and shaking hands with the Irish Spaniard and my fists at the Spanish one, I set off and joined my Regiment in a dirty village called Ahetze about eleven at night after fourteen hours' ride. Beverley left me at St Jean de Luz.

My captain, who seizes every opportunity of making me miserable because I will not bow to his hauteur, received me in the German manner and we all four sleep in one room each having his bundle of straw in the respective corners. The house is situated in a thick wood and we have lost sight of the French.

Rainy, cold and mist. My ankle strengthens.

8 December   This is a sketch of the house in which we are quartered at Ahetze and from which I wrote a day or two ago to Henry, Lotherington and Brookes [Plate 5b, *facing p.* 16].

[*Victory on the Nivelle had taken the Allied army forward to the Nive. The French, leaving St Jean de Luz and twelve hundred prisoners in Wellington's hands, had been forced back towards Bayonne. Their losses had been twice as heavy as those of the relentlessly advancing and now highly confident army.*

Sir John Hope's left wing, only tentatively engaged, had suffered little. Most of his casualties, as at the Bidassoa, were incurred by the German Legion and, also as at the Bidassoa, by the light battalions. The line battalions had lost one officer (Boyd) and eleven men killed, and two officers (one of whom was Wheatley) and fifty-five men wounded.

Wheatley had been back with his battalion for less than a week when he was on the move again.

The resumed advance entailed a considerable risk, for the Nive was flooded and crossing it would be a necessarily slow operation. There would be a dangerous period, before it was bridged, when the army would be divided and Soult, whose forces were concentrated round Bayonne, would be able to throw his full strength at either part.

Wellington, nevertheless, having great faith in his men, resolved to make an attempt at forcing a passage.

Again Hope's left wing were to stage a false attack along the coast, while five divisions were to cross the river farther inland – Rowland Hill's three divisions (one British, one Spanish and one Portuguese) at Cambo, Beresford's two British divisions at Ustaritz – and then, leaving men to build bridges, all five divisions were to sweep round towards Bayonne.

On 9 December the first part of the plan was carried out.[1]]

9 December[2] At five this morning, just as I was in bed, we were suddenly aroused to march instantly. And after three hours' walk in the dark across roads and fields we entered the high road, choked up with troops.

As soon as day broke an instantaneous firing began and a sharp battle ensued [*with units from the divisions of Generals Boyer and Leval*]. At one part of the fight I was so far advanced on the high road [*near Anglet*] as to perceive the steeples of Bayonne with the fortified camp [*of Beyris*] and this harrassing fight lasted till dark.

Saw Carmichael's brother[3] wounded in the bend of the arm; and met in the heat of the firing great fat Macbean[4] with a ball in the palm of his hand, as pale as the ghost of Hamlet.

We drove the French three miles back; and after standing over large fires until eleven at night, the rains fell so heavy that they all went out.

1. A plan to illustrate the Battle of the Nive will be found on p. 91.
2. The date in the Diary is given as 10 December, but the operations Wheatley describes took place on 9 December. All the dates between 9 December and 17 December have accordingly been brought back a day to tally with the entries.
3. If he was an officer, he was not apparently in the King's German Legion. He may have been Ensign Thomas Carmichael of the 47th or Lieutenant Lewis Carmichael of the 59th. The 2nd Battalions of both these regiments were in the 5th Division.
4. Lieutenant Alexander Macbean, 2nd Light Battalion K.G.L. His name was spelled Maclean in the 1814 Army List; but the mistake was corrected in the 1815 List.

[The day's operations had been performed without much difficulty. Hill and Beresford had both managed to force the Nive, and Hope's left wing, as Wheatley says, had pushed the French outposts back towards Bayonne.

At nightfall, however, Sir John Hope, who was not at his best during this battle, sent back the 5th Division to Bidart and Guéthary and the 1st Division almost as far back as St Jean de Luz. Wheatley's battalion withdrew to its camp at Ahetze. The ground that had been won was left in the hands of small pickets from the Portuguese brigades. Hope was clearly not expecting the strong counterattack that Soult was preparing.]

In the course of an hour we set off for our old quarters, the sand and mud above our ankles. My foot and thigh were so excessively painful that I sank on the ground quite spiritless and as Llewellyn's company passed I cried out for him when he humanely stopped and assisted me home.

Both ignorant of the way we came, we did not reach Ahetze before six in the morning where we found the whole Regiment under arms.

Nötting cries out on seeing me, 'Well, Sir, I thought you had deserted!'

'Your thoughts, Sir,' I answered, 'like yourself, are good for nothing.'

I'm certain this fellow will do his utmost to get rid of me some way or other in the course of this campaign but I'll wait for an opportunity and shew him that tame as I am by disposition, I will never brook the contumely of the haughty and ignorant.

10 December Left Ahetze in toto about eleven o'clock A.M. A sharp firing on our left *[from Lord Aylmer's brigade who were advancing to the support of the Allied pickets driven back by Soult's counterattack]*.

About one o'clock halted in a field in Battle array in sight of the battle which lasted till night. Stood all night in this field. Wet and windy.

[Soon after the arrival of the 1st Division, tired by their long march up the sodden coast from St Jean de Luz, the battle had dwindled away into a skirmish. Lord Aylmer's brigade, the Portuguese brigades and the 5th Division had averted the danger of a French breakthrough. Neither the Guards brigade nor the German Legion were employed.]

11 December Stood the entire day waiting for the word to advance.

Was desired by Colonel Ompteda to carry the Standard when ordered to engage.

Slept in a ditch with Llewellyn and Vassmer.[1] Nothing to eat. Wet. In great pain.

[The 5th Division and Aylmer's brigade again took the brunt of the fighting, the Guards and the Germans being still in support. Only when the fighting died down did Hope replace the exhausted 5th Division by the 1st.]

12 December   Sharp fighting again.

[The 5th Line Battalion, however, was never seriously engaged. It suffered no casualties this day. The Guards brigade, though, had 180 casualties, most of them incurred during an artillery duel.]

The French fell back to Bayonne.

[Soult had decided to transfer his attack to Rowland Hill's 14,000 troops on the other side of the Nive at St Pierre. This attack took place the following day. Although heavily outnumbered, Hill's men held their ground until Wellington reinforced them. The French were eventually repulsed. The 1st Division took no part in this action.]

13 December   On outlying piquet. Fatigue excessive.

14 December   On outlying piquet by the Mayor's House *[the Mayor of the village of Biarritz who lived at Barouillet]* on the hill. This is the fifth night I've had my feet wet and without rest. Miserable and half-starved. Cold and windy.

15 December   Relieved from piquet and marched back to quarters at Guéthary near the shore.

16 December   Fine day, walked with Drysdale,[2] Gardner[3] and Llewellyn over the fields – full of dead. Saw horrible sights. Horrid trade.

25 December   On outlying piquet near the Mayor's house on the

---

1. Ensign Henry Vassmer, 5th Line Battalion K.G.L.
2. Lieutenant William Drysdale, 1st Line Battalion K.G.L. He was badly wounded at Bayonne the following April.
3. Ensign Patrick Gardner, 2nd Line Battalion K.G.L.

high road. Each battalion takes its turn which comes round every third day. Nothing but tobacco and brandy this Christmas day. A day of mirth and feasting in old England. Fine sharp weather. The bay boisterous.

27 December Crowds of people came out from Bayonne and they say the paving from the streets is taken up which is generally considered the forerunner of obstinate resistance. Met Lord Wellington. He looked pale and harrassed.

28 December Removed to the sea shore. Nötting and I in one room where I write this. Wind and thunder.

1814

1 January 1814 At Guéthary. The Paris paper mentions our being in want of provisions. But good bread and meat delivered daily. The Army healthy and hearty. Fresh meat in abundance. The rice which is sometimes given to the army is Lord Wellington's gift.

4 January Headquarters at St Jean de Luz. The Legion appears anxious to return to Germany after nine years' tedious absence. Even the short period I have been absent from England appears treble the time.

11 January Nothing particular has transpired since Christmas. The line is the same as before, excepting the 5th Division has gone more to the Centre and the left flank consists of Lord Aylmer's brigade. The weather just now resembles that of Old England. Rain, snow, cold and sleet. The village is named Guéthary. Dirty place.

'Tis amusing to see the sudden change of dress between the women of Gascony and Biscay. Every female wears a red crossed handkerchief on the head on this side the water. I've already roughly sketched the Biscay lasses and in the next page I'll give a Gascon Paysanne. One can see how gradually they become more *à la Française*. Singular that a small river should create so great a distinction!

All country people wear the same dress and all appear of one school or public institution. So diametrically opposite to our British customs where every one dresses different according to fancy!

The Paysans of Gascony wear wooden shoes. Wove caps of Bayonne are universally worn by the inhabitants of this County and sketches give their shape and form [*Figure 1*].

Fig. 1. *'One can see how gradually they become more* à la Française'

The lasses are up with the sun, and ten or twelve of them are seen skipping along the road with milk and butter, singing and laughing as unconcernedly as if all was peace and tranquility; and when receiving their scanty demand for their articles of commerce they smile upon the hand which probably has curtailed some beloved relative's existence or is predestined to destroy the being of one dearer than relationship, for the French Emperor has seized all capable of carrying arms and none but females and aged men are to be met with here.

[Nearly all the diaries and letters of the period mention the friendliness of the civilian population, whose goodwill Wellington was determined to keep, for he could not spare the troops to fight partisans or to guard his supplies and lines of communication. Such troops were never required. The British, made to behave well and to pay for what they needed, were

30

welcomed almost as liberators by the Gascons, who had been treated by the French army in a far less considerate way.

If this, one English officer thought, was what campaigning in an enemy country was like, he never wanted to campaign in a friendly one again.[1]

This happy relationship between the French civilians and the invading army had not, of course, been achieved without difficulty. The depredations of the troops after crossing the frontier had at first been appalling. One private, tried and hanged for rape, explained that 'as he was now in France he thought it must be in order'.[2] *And the Spanish and Portuguese troops behaved quite as badly as Wellington had feared, and had to be sent back across the border. 'They seemed verily to have pledged themselves to wreak vengeance on France, and to repay her for all she had done to them', wrote August Schaumann. 'Their eyes were aflame. Every Frenchman who fell into their hands was ill-treated or secretly murdered. Before leaving a village they always plundered it and set it on fire. All the inhabitants were taking flight. Even the men of our legion, remembering the ill-treatment Hanover had been forced to suffer, fancied themselves called upon to make reprisals on the French. But Lord Wellington, who was clever enough to see whither such behaviour would lead, issued one or two furious general orders, and constituting his brother-in-law, General Pakenham,*[3] *head of the military police, gave him the most stringent and solemn instructions to hang without trial or mercy any who was caught red-handed in* actu flagrante. *Pakenham, supported by a powerful guard and the provost-marshal, then began to ride up and down our columns like a raving lion seeking whom he might devour. His command, "Let that scoundrel be hanged instantly!" was executed in a twinkling ... I saw the body of a Spanish muleteer, who had entered a house to steal apples, hanging from the window of that house as a warning to all marauders. In his mouth, which had fallen open in the process of strangulation, they had stuck an apple to show what he had coveted!'*

Within a short time such punishments had restored discipline and Schaumann's 'hosts and the whole neighbourhood could not cease from singing the praises of our army, and of its good behaviour and discipline'.[4]

On Sunday evenings the Girls dance, sing and play the tambourine. Very shy of Englishmen.

1. Sir Arthur Bryant, *The Age of Elegance* (Collins, 1950), 81–83.
2. Bryant, *op. cit.*, 82.
3. Major-General Hon. Sir Edward Pakenham was the brother of Wellington's wife.
4. Schaumann, *op. cit.*, 394–5, 402.

In Biscay when making parties of pleasure the Girls saddle a strong horse or mule and, one counterbalancing the other, jog along the road with their galants in holiday suits firing their muskets, showing feats of agility and cutting capers like so many monkies. 'Tis astonishing what power women have over us and what fools we become at times!! *'Oh, tempora! Oh, mores!'*[1]

Not having been in the interior I dare not make any observation on the Gentry excepting the Basques. The Ladies attend worship in deep mourning with black veils over their heads. They wear no bonnets and their hair being tastefully dressed, the veil covers them to the knees. Their carriage is excellent and their shape exquisite. The Commonalty wear black hoods of coarse cloth entirely enveloping the head and shoulders; and the service being mostly kneeling the tout-ensemble is sombre, striking and romantic.

The Basque language a monotony of sound. Never could catch a word.[2]

24 January Frosty just now. The Pyrenees covered with snow and the wind so strong I can almost lean against it.

27 January Dreadful storm in the Bay of Biscay. The waves throw every moment large pieces of timber and broken furniture on shore. A ship wrecked on the beach this morning was covered with wax candles. Took myself a lump of fresh butter, about three lbs. – a great rarity. About half a mile towards St Jean de Luz, a young lady in black with silk stockings on was dashed on shore by the relentless

---

1. Since Wheatley wrote his diary for his beloved Eliza, he does not, of course, mention any love affairs or sexual adventures. The diary of August Schaumann, which was not written under such a handicap as Wheatley's was, reveals that Allied officers were rarely deprived for long of the pleasures of female society. Schaumann himself, so he said, had had 'plenty of love affairs in Spain'. In one town alone he had affairs with five different women at once. Two of these women were the daughters of a wealthy landowner and were 'very responsive', one was the wife of a Spanish colonel, the fourth a pretty girl who paid him 'many visits, and the fifth the legitimate spouse of an organist, who always availed herself of her husband's duties in the church' in order to come to him. He was not so lucky, he admitted, with the Basque girls, and had to console himself with the 'beauties among the soldiers' wives'. – Schaumann, *op. cit.* 386, 388. Schaumann's claims were not exceptional.

2. 'As this language bears no resemblance to any other language either living or dead,' wrote August Schaumann, 'it was utterly incomprehensible to us. It is said to be the language spoken by Tubal, Noah's nephew, who came to Spain 143 years after the Flood.' – Schaumann, *op. cit.*, 382. – Basque is, indeed, isolated from the other languages of Europe though having grammatical affinities with the Magyar and Finnish languages.

Plate 7 'A set of infernal-looking beings.'

Plate 8 'We found a church before us, behind the walls of which were crowds of heads.' – the Church of St Etienne, half a mile north of Bayonne.

waves.[1] Buried in the Town. *'Mors omnibus communis.'* Dreadful hurricane still.

28 January All still in front.

[*It was all still on most other parts of the front, too. Indeed, on both sides during these last months of the war officers and men alike were anxious to avoid 'unnecessary waste of life in petty outpost bickering'. Not only was there very little interference with sentries once the two lines of pickets had been laid out, but there was a great deal of fraternization, though this applied less to Spanish and Portuguese regiments and the K.G.L. than to British regiments. To shoot an exposed sentry was unthinkable, and if a French or British officer thought an enemy outpost was too far forward he preferred to send a message through the hedge or across the stream that divided the two armies with a request that the outpost be moved farther back. Often cheerful conversations were carried on in pidgin-Spanish and the bartering of food and liquor was common. Many pleasant stories are told of the friendly relations that existed between the two armies. Once a bullock, issued as rations to a French regiment, escaped from the butcher and charged into the British lines. A French delegation came over and begged to have it back, as they had been without meat for a week; so the English soldiers sent half of it back with a bucket of loaves as compensation for the rest and with the apology that they had felt obliged to cut the animal in half as beef was 'not too common' in their quarters either. And once a company of riflemen 'clubbed half a dollar' each to send a man across to the French to buy brandy. The representative unfortunately sampled so much of his large purchases that he was incapable of carrying the remainder back, and the French had to shout for the other members of the syndicate to come and get him. It was not impossible, apparently, to find a sentry with French and English muskets slung over his shoulder guarding a bridge on behalf of both armies!*]

29 January The weather still inclement. The wind boisterous. The surf is very heavy all along from the Bidassoa to the Adour, the shore being rocky as the sailors term it. Am ordered to bathe my ankle in the sea every morning. The Piquets are not so strong just now as heretofore. I prognosticate peace before the 26 of July 1814. Fine

1. 'A ship-cable with the G.R. was found at Bidart, and three men and a woman. Some say the latter had silk stockings on. One body cast up here was half eaten, and I saw a backbone only yesterday. The bodies of mules float in and out every tide.' – Larpent, ii, 280.

Noyau[1] in this town of Guéthary. There are thirty-six men lodged over our room and the perpetual tramping is a fine relief to a meditative mind.

A telegraphic communication is adopted when the army is in winter quarters and the one in use with us is at the Mayor's house. This is the sketch taken when on duty with it last week [*Figure 2*].

Fig. 2 *'My written orders were if a disturbance appeared among the enemy to lift one flag'*

My written orders were if a disturbance appeared among the enemy to lift one flag; if the French piquets retired, two flags; if they fired at me, three flags. At night if they began to be clamorous or retreat to hoist the tub of pitch and set fire to it. If they endeavoured to advance, to fire my tent and a bonfire near it and to retreat as well as I could to the rere piquets. On any signal made thus a cannon, half a mile back, fired and was answered by another to Guéthary and so back to St Jean de Luz where Lord Wellington lives.[2]

When on piquet some days at this telegraph with Corporal Einer and three men, about one o'clock in the morning I was reading in my tent when who should come in but Llewellyn. Surprised at this early

1. 'A liqueur made from brandy flavoured with the kernels of certain nuts.' – *O.E.D.*
2. 'We have now established a sort of little telegraph of signals to the right and in front, to let Lord Wellington know immediately if anything is going forward.' – Larpent, *op. cit.*, ii, 233.

visit and more so when he enquired where the Sentry was and said that no body was round the fire, out I sallied with a candle and found the Sentry dead drunk and Corporal Einer insensible by the fire with one man and the other missing. All the kicking possible could not revive them and I was obliged to stand Sentry myself till day break, Llewellyn cooking the coffee.

On arousing Corporal Einer I discovered a couple of muleteers had been treating them with aqua dentae, a bottle of which I discovered under some furze.

About eight o'clock, seeing a light horseman coming by, I desired him to look over the heath and after a fatiguing search I found [the missing man] in a bush stripped naked and frozen to death. Not knowing how to conceal this unpleasant business from the Colonel (as death to them all is the result of sleeping upon Duty before the enemy, and having once been guilty of the same myself) I determined to screen the poor fellows. So digging a deep hole we buried the man and I reported him as having deserted to the enemy. The other three would go to the Devil for me now. But should it be discovered, I shall go to him myself I fear.

I cannot vouch for its being the general Custom to bury the dead in this manner in Gascony but I've seen several in this way without mourners [*Figure 3*].

Fig. 3   *'I've seen several in this way without mourners'*

Spanish segars are very good but very strong. They are dear – 2s. 6d the three dozen. French Noyau excellent – 1½ dollar the bottle. Champaigne, 3 dollars the bottle. Port Wine, one dollar.

The French muskets are not so heavy nor so lasting as ours.[1]

1. The French musket was inferior to the English, for not only did it throw a lighter ball, but the coarse powder used necessitated washing out the barrel twice as often.

Their bayonets fasten on with a screw or spring. Their hats are iron bound and may be called everlasting. The soldiers are pretty well dressed but I cannot vouch for their being so well fed, as rumours are so numerous. Their physiognomy is pleasing, I think.

29 January A violent storm. Hail, snow, rain, etc. No news from the front.

30 January On piquet at the Mayor's house.

9 February Nothing particular has transpired lately.

10 February The Duke d'Angouleme at Headquarters.[1] Frosty and snow.

19 February This morning we left Guéthary and after three hours cross marching encamped in a large turnip field on the left of the high road near the village of Biarritz, a watering place on the sea shore.

20 February On outlying piquet at a small ruined house on the left of the highroad in sight of Bayonne.

21 February This morning when the sun rose 'twas a fine frosty morning and Bacmeister, the Captain on piquet with me, asked me to reconnoitre the enemy with him as was the Captain's duty before the relief of the piquet. We cross'd the [felled] trees laying across the high road and taking a rifleman with us, we walked slowly and cautiously without seeing a frenchman.

Bacmeister then crept behind the hedge on the left, I on the right and the rifleman in the high road, and the devil of a frenchman could we see. The Bayonne bells were ringing merrily.

1. Louis-Antoine de Bourbon, Duc d'Angoulême, elder son of the Comte d'Artois. Napoleon's defeats in 1813 had revived the hopes of the royalists, and Wellington himself believed that if a Prince of the House of Bourbon came forward 'in the field in France; and if Great Britain would stand by him I am certain he would succeed'. – *Despatches*, XI, 306. But when Angoulême came to St Jean de Luz (where Wellington's headquarters was now) on 2 February he did not create a very favourable impression.

'I do not think much of the little Duke', Larpent wrote. 'His figure and manners are by no means imposing, and I think his talents are not very great.' – Larpent, *op. cit.*, ii, 288.

As soon as he arrived at Bordeaux he felt obliged to ask for a guard to protect him from his own countrymen.

Plate 9 'That rascal Nötting desired me to enter the house with fifteen men, while he stood behind.'

KEY : 1, *The Room at the back. 2, Captain Nötting. 3, The Citadel. 4, Bayonne. 5, French batteries.*

Plate 10 'The steeple fell with a horrible crash.'

At last, before we came to a turn in the road the soldier said he heard the clattering of horses. Getting through the hedge, I put my ear to the pavement and heard horses footsteps clearly. We had too far to retreat, so broke through the hedge again and lay quietly down, and peeping through the hedge saw a Serjeant and six men trot by, as far as our first Sentry.

With what anxiety we expected their return! After remaining a full hour in this miserable position, Bacmeister called from over the road to desire me and the man to return as cautiously as possible and he would follow, which we did and gained at last the felled tree. The sentry there informed us the French patrol had turned to the left. This is the last time I will volunteer to oblige a fellow who fears doing his duty alone.

[*The fighting south and east of Bayonne during the second week of December 1813 had dispirited the French troops and caused them further heavy casualties. Soult had been obliged to abandon all hope of a counter-attack and had been forced back on to the defensive. In order to keep open the Adour river on which he had to rely for his communications with central France, he had adopted a wide front stretching from Bayonne in the west to Peyrehorade (where his own headquarters now was) twenty-two miles to the east. Four divisions – those of Leval, Abbé, Taupin and Maransin – he left in Bayonne, under the command of General Honoré Reille; three divisions – Foy's, Boyer's and Darmagnac's – were between Bayonne and Peyrehorade; and two others – Daricau's and a newly formed division under General Harispe – were south of the Adour on Wellington's right flank ready to attack him from that side when he advanced to force a passage of the lower Adour.*

This, however, was not Wellington's intention. He meant instead to strike eastwards into the interior with the larger part of his army and then having, as he hoped, drawn Soult's attention to his threatened flank, send Sir John Hope's divisions against his other flank and across the upper Adour between Bayonne and the sea.

Wellington had been aware since 10 January that the Austrian, Prussian and Russian armies had crossed the Rhine and, although he disapproved of their method of advance, he knew that he must soon act in support of them. A month later, several days' sunshine having dried the roads and Napoleon having withdrawn 14,000 of Soult's men – including Leval's division from Bayonne – for his own operation in the north, Wellington decided to resume his advance. By 19 February Soult's forces east of Bayonne had been pushed back as far as the Gave d'Oloron. Now was the time for Hope's divisions to act.]

22 February Left tents standing and entered the village of Biarritz. Just as I had got into bed and was asleep, about twelve o'clock, we were ordered to march instantly. The night was cold and dreary. After about six hours' walking, three persons on horseback overtook us on an immense heath. As they rode by, one asked what Regiment [we were] and where we were going. The Colonel told him and that we had no guide, and he led us till day break. We then discovered our leader [to be] the hero of Salamanca, the conqueror of Vitoria – Lord Wellington.

[Wellington, who had been conducting the operations east of Bayonne, had returned to St Jean de Luz on 19 February to help Sir John Hope get his men across the estuary west of the town. But the gales which Wheatley describes had prevented the luggers that were to have bridged the estuary from coming up from St Jean de Luz and Socoa, and two days later Wellington left Hope to manage as best he could when the gales subsided and he returned to the Gave d'Oloron front.

He returned, in fact, on the morning of 21 February before the 5th Line Battalion had left Biarritz, so that the senior officer who guided Colonel Ompteda past Anglet towards the Adour cannot have been Wellington, as Wheatley supposed.]

23 February On the sand of the banks of the Adour where we bivouacked all day and slept all night. Cold and frosty and starry.

[The wind had fallen at last and the luggers had been ordered to put out to sea and sail for the mouth of the Adour. But before they reached it, the wind changed and they were blown off course. Hope, nevertheless, decided to try to get across the estuary by means of the pontoons and small boats which he had got with him.

Giving orders for Lord Aylmer's brigade, the Portuguese and Spanish brigades and the K.G.L. light infantry brigade of the 1st Division to simulate an attack on the entrenched camps south of Bayonne, he sent the Guards forward to lead the river crossing.]

24 February Half a regiment of the Guards having crossed over last night, the tide became so rapid that twas dangerous to attempt to join them. About two o'clock this morning a body from Bayonne [*the 5th Léger and the 62nd Ligne*] attacked these poor fellows. The utmost distress prevailed. Our Artillery fired across the river at random. At last a brigade of Congreve rockets pelting among them, they desisted. One rocket cut down twenty-three men at once.

[Congreve rockets, invented by the ingenious Sir William Congreve (1772–1828), whose talents were much admired by the Prince Regent, had been first used in an attack on Boulogne in 1806 and later at the siege of Copenhagen and in the Walcheren expedition. The French troops at Bayonne were, however, unused to them; and the deafening noise they made, combined with the unexpectedly good aim of the rocketeers who had crossed the Adour with the Guards, contributed much to the success of Sir John Hope's daring adventure.

According to Lieutenant-Colonel Julius von Hartman of the K.G.L. artillery, the rocket-guns were fired with such 'striking effect that the enemy at once retreated in great confusion. The rocket-gunners went after the enemy, and there was now beheld the extraordinary spectacle of strong masses of war-hardened infantry giving way without resistance to a dozen opponents. So deep, indeed, was the feeling of dread created by this new and alarming weapon, that the French columns could not be brought to a stand till they had reached the Citadel.'[1]

In letters to his wife Lieutenant-Colonel Sir Augustus Frazer, of the Royal Horse Artillery, writes of the prejudice against Congreve rockets that existed in the Army. The prejudice was shared by Wellington. 'I don't want to set fire to any town,' he wrote home, 'and I don't know any other use of rockets.' At a demonstration of them which he attended they 'did not seem to answer very well', according to F. S. Larpent, the Judge Advocate-General. 'They certainly made a most tremendous noise, and were formidable spitfires – no cavalry could stand if they came near them, but there seemed the difficulty, none went within half a mile of the intended object, and the direction seemed excessively uncertain. The ground was very bad, and on a flat, or along a road, where they would ricochet or bound along straight they might do very well, but in our case they went bang into the ground . . . some pieces of the shell came back even amongst us spectators.'[2]

But Colonel Frazer, who was also disappointed at first, carried out further tests, 'firing a good many and in various ways', and eventually

---

1. Quoted by Louis von Ompteda, *op. cit.*
2. Larpent, *op. cit.*, ii, 256–7; see also W. H. Maxwell, *op. cit.*, 165.

decided that they 'answered well enough'. He had no doubt that they would prove 'useful on the Adour'.[1] *And he was right.*

As well as being helped by the rockets, Hope was helped, too, of course, by the inability of the French generals at Bayonne to understand what was happening, for Reille was no longer in command there. After Leval's division had been withdrawn east by Soult – leaving only Abbé's division in support of the garrison – Reille refused to be left in Bayonne with the Governor, General Thouvenot, and had resigned his command. Thouvenot was not equal to taking it up. He had withdrawn the French outpost and small battery on the north bank of the Adour estuary at Le Boucau before the attack, confident that he was not threatened on that side; and even after the Guards had got several companies on to the north bank he made no more energetic effort to dislodge them than the sending of an order to General Maucomble in the Citadel to 'reconnoitre the troops that had crossed.']

About three P.M. I crossed in a pontoon.

If the men do not sit still the boat begins to rock and the motion increases of itself until the whole are in imminent Danger.

We slept this night on the sand and had nothing to eat. Very cold and frosty. Fine weather.

25 February Marched early and encamped on the Bordeaux road, one mile from Bayonne near Boucau and Tarnos. Fine and frosty.

26 February In Camp. The French Girls sell us eggs and butter.

27 February About eleven o'clock this morning while sitting at the Gaming table with Linsingen[2] and Korschann[3] and Rothhard[4] a strong cannonading began at a distance, and suddenly a cry of 'Fall in!' broke up the party. The men were ordered to load their muskets and we set off directly. Descending a hill we wound round a lake and ascending a hill went through an orchard. Presently a ball whizzed over us, then another. Running forward, we dashed on and soon saw crowds of

1. *Letters of Colonel Sir Augustus Simon Frazer, K.C.B.*, edited by Major-General Edward Sabine (1859), 392, 403.
2. Lieutenant Charles, Baron Linsingen, 5th Line Battalion. He had several relatives in the King's German Legion, including Lieutenant-General Baron Linsingen, who was Colonel Commandant of the 1st Regiment of Light Dragoons.
3. Lieutenant Joseph Korschann, 5th Line Battalion K.G.L.
4. Lieutenant Adolphus Rothhard, 5th Line Battalion K.G.L.

enemies. They would not meet our bayonets but scampered off. Our battalion ran into a narrow bye road, the 1st Battalion before us, and soon gaining the end of the lane we found a Church before us, behind the walls of which were crowds of heads (Plate 8, *facing p. 33*].

[*Having got a bridge of boats across the Adour estuary on 26 February, Hope had now managed to bring fifteen thousand British troops on to the northern bank and had encircled Bayonne. Before formal siege could be laid to the fortress, however, it was necessary to close up on to the Citadel which dominated the town from the northern bank of the Adour. This operation involved the storming of all the minor fortifications round the base of the Citadel hill in the suburbs of St Etienne. The K.G.L. brigades, supported by the Guards and the Portuguese, were given this task.*]

The battle of St Etienne was dreadfully hot. The men and officers fell thick and frequent. A pole firing across my face received a ball through his chest and fell upon me so heavily that my knees sank and I dropped on my back. The closeness of the place was very unfavourable to us and I advised Nötting to run forward. At the same instant Colonel Ompteda, rushing forward, thundered out a charge and we scaled the churchyard walls after an obstinate resistance. The instant I got over I ran up to a french man who stood motionless and then fell on his knees. In the act of collaring him, a cannon ball from the Citadel split the tree the other side of the wall and one of the splinters knocked my hat off. Llewellyn just then ran up with intent to kill the French man but I guarded him and gave him in charge.

We all took shelter inside the Church until further orders and the smashing of the windows from the balls together with the thunder of the Cannon in a peacable room like a church, quite bewildered me.

The three first companies of the 5th Battalion were soon ordered out. Colonel Ompteda leading us, we ran down the lane we had come up, and turning afterwards to the left down a narrow lane, found ourselves on the high road, close to the grand entrance into Bayonne.

On the right hand side stood a shoemaker's shop and Colonel Ompteda ordered the Grenadiers to seize it and defend it to the last extremity.

The occurence I now proceed to relate displays so much german malice and dastardly enmity that I cannot refrain being a little prolix in the narration. [It] evidently shews that even in the moment of inevitable destruction some minds are so tainted with a deadly spite

41

that even death's ghastly stare cannot for a moment eradicate the baneful venom.

The house we were ordered to defend faced all the batteries of Bayonne looking to the north and the Citadel stared it in the face. On turning to the right and breaking through a little Garden, we got near the back kitchen in a yard where the water tubs stood. Here we mustered the Company. [There were] about thirty only remaining. That rascal Nötting called up Schauroth[1] and myself, the Youngest officer, and desired me to enter the house with fifteen men while he stood behind to assist in the yard with Schauroth. The following is a sketch of the house [Plate 9, *facing p. 36*].

On getting in and fastening downstairs, I took the Serjeant and my men up stairs and I found the top divided into three rooms in one row with a narrow passage leading to the whole. The front rooms faced Bayonne and the passage looked into the Yard where Captain Nötting and Schauroth stood.

Putting the Serjeant and six men in the left room and four in each of the others, I superintended the whole and began by firing the first shot myself.

My poor fellows did their utmost. The French scorned our musketry at first and only returned it in the same coin [after] about ten minutes. I lost two killed from the centre room and one in [the] right hand one.

Colonel Ompteda and two English Artillery Officers came up and enquired for me. I was in the act of firing from the third room as he came in, desiring me to mind the men that they elevated their fire-arms properly.

In about two hours more I had sent two wounded away from the left [room] and had one more killed in the Centre [room]. Just at this time the French poured in grape at us and one or two forty-eight pounders which filled the rooms with mortar dust and we fired back at random. The top of my military cap was taken off by a cannon shot and smashed against the wall. Just then a violent scream from the next room, with a thundering noise announced the corners of the house being blown down.

Desiring Lather, the shoe-maker of our Company and the only [man] left in the Centre room, to stand his ground, I ran out to keep the men in; and as I turned to the right I bawled into the yard, 'Send

1. Lieutenant George de Schauroth, 5th Line Battalion K.G.L. He was wounded soon afterwards.

up some more men.' But my eyes were so full of dust that I could see no one and the noise so great, perhaps, they could not hear.

I had just at this time the narrowest escape of all. I was leaning against the wall opposite the Centre room, rubbing my eyes and collecting my senses, so horrible was the noise, when the Serjeant from the [other] room tapped me on the Shoulder, saying, 'Sir, Martin is shot in the head.'

I had not taken two steps to the left to proceed to the room when an immense sixty-eight pounder poured through the house and made a hole large enough to jump through in the very spot I had that instant left.

My men were now so few that I saw it would be useless. However I returned to the Centre room where Lather alone was, and after firing till my shoulder was black and blue, the French poured in so strongly upon us that I began to think of leaving the house as the Serjeant had advised me.

The two corners of the house were laid open and near one hundred and thirty cannons pointing at us. My men were reduced from fifteen to five and the Serjeant. And I was just making up my mind when a confusion as if heaven and earth were in contact suddenly came over me. The roof fell in and buried the whole of us.

As Lather and myself were in the middle place, we fell together. My left elbow was so nearly smashed that I carry my arm in a sling. The Shoe-maker's head was actually scalped and when I groped into the yard like a miller the Captain says, 'I thought you was killed, Wheatley. Where is the Company?'

'You will see them again,' I answered, 'and I hope shortly.'

'Why, where are they, then, Sir?'

'Gone to hell!'

The Serjeant and three men were all that escaped and if I live a thousand years I shall never forget this day's work, nor Mr Nötting's friendship.

One poor fellow came rushing out from the ruins raving mad with his thigh crushed to a jelly. We could scarce hold him. He died that evening.

Nötting gave me some rum which he found in the house below; and it being dark we remained on Piquet all night.

28 February Skirmishing all day. Faint. Went to the hospital, got my elbow poulticed by Gerson. Visiting my shattered house in the evening with Llewellyn, I found among some rubbish the Queen of Prussia's Waltz. Rainy.

On the 27th my Regiment lost one hundred and fifty men and seven Officers hors de Combat. [*According to the official return the 5th Line Battalion, which suffered more heavily than any other, lost 106 men and 7 officers – no doubt several men at first reported missing later returned to their companies.*] Linsingen, Korschann and Rothhard, who were all playing at Cards with me the morning before Yesterday, are seriously wounded.

We have now pitched our Camp near the high road where I write this on the damp ground.

[*This fierce fighting in the northern suburbs of Bayonne had cost the King's German Legion no less than 371 casualties in all, most of them in the line battalions which had been given the task of assaulting the centre of the enemy's lines at St Etienne. In addition to the three officers whom Wheatley mentions, his friend Drysdale and Schauroth were also wounded, as was General von Hinüber. Despite the valuable and heroic service performed by the K.G.L., however, no mention was made of them in the official dispatch which Wellington sent to Earl Bathurst on 1 March, 'an omission somewhat remarkable because Hope had openly commended their valour'.[1] Hinüber complained of this to the Adjutant-General, the Hon. Sir Edward Pakenham, in a letter a copy of which he sent to Adolphus Frederick, Duke of Cambridge, who was colonel-in-chief of the Corps.*

Pakenham replied to the just complaint in a letter which Hinüber describes as being 'as cold a letter as ever issued from an office'. This is it:

'Dear Sir,

I mentioned to my lord Wellington the sentiments expressed in your letter of the 25th ultimo, and am desired to observe that his excellency has ever had pleasure in being satisfied with the conduct of the legion, during the service of the corps composing it under his orders. I am in no way authorized to enter into further explanation on the subject to which your communication relates, but I would recommend you to subdue any anxiety that may have arisen on account of his excellency's good opinion of the legion, which he has always taken occasion to express, when called upon to speak of the corps.

1. Napier, *op. cit.*, vi, 95.

Plate 11 'An accurate likeness of his drunken face.' – Henry Llewellyn.

Plate 12 'It stood the cannonading of Bayonne without any impression being made on it.' – The windmill at St Etienne.

*I have the honor to be
Dear Sir,
Your very obedient servant,
Edward Pakenham
Adjutant-General.'*[1]

There the matter seems to have rested.]

*

10 April We have now been piquetting for two months before this infernal fortress [*Bayonne*] endeavouring to starve them out, while we are in want of food ourselves. For nothing but herrings and brandy are come-attable. Our tents are pitched by a large swamp and the French pour in cannon shot and shells every ten minutes among us.

The duty is harrassing: On Monday on piquet in the Church of St Etienne, on Tuesday on the support near the Church, on Wednesday all night digging in the entrenchments near the Windmill, on Friday in the Church again, and so on.

When sitting round the fire [in the church] one night a ball entered the door, passed through the aisle over the men's heads, and split the altar into a thousand pieces, without injuring a single person.

Llewellyn one day climbed up into the roof and discovered the whole church paraphanalia of flowers, candlesticks, etc., which he was compelled to replace to prevent religious disputes among the Poles.

On Easter Sunday, about three o'clock in the Afternoon all being very still – more so than usual – we peeped out and perceived the batteries lined with ladies and gentlemen. Surprised, I strolled with Stratton of the Sappers and Miners[2] a little forward, when suddenly the whole Citadel began a tremendous cannonading on the unfortunate steeple of St Etienne and after four hundred or more balls had passed through it, it fell with a horrible crash [Plate 10, *facing p. 37*]. The fools in the fortress gave loud huzzas and the ladies retired delighted with the afternoon's entertainment. Then all became quiet as the grave again.

The windmill near St Etienne was bomb- and ball-proof. It stood the cannonading of Bayonne without any impression being made upon it, though once a cannon ball entered the door and took off the left knee of Private Ludolf of the Light Company. We were at last

1. Beamish, *op. cit.*, ii, App. xiv, E.
2. Sub-Lieutenant William Stratton, the Corps of Royal Sappers and Miners.

45

compelled to take it down for want of firewood [Plate 12, *facing p. 45*].

The hospitals are filled with sick, among whom is Llewellyn. My boots have been on since the 27th of February and my shirt also.

We lose men daily, and if this lasts much longer I fear I shall increase the number in the hospital as my knees are a little swelled and stiff. Saw my baggage this morning for the first time. I think tis Hotspur who said: 'By heavens, methinks it were an easy leap to pluck bright honour from the pale-fac'd moon or dive into the bottom of the deep where fathom-line could never touch the ground and pluck up drowned honour by the locks.'[1] Hotspur never blockaded Bayonne.

11 April Lieutenant Henry Llewellyn of the 5th Line Battalion King's German Legion. An accurate likeness of his drunken face as taken by Edmund Wheatley of the same Regiment this morning, April 11th, on his return from the hospital at Boucau. Vivant Rex et Regina [Plate 11, *facing p. 44*].

14 April Last night the 47th and two other Regiments[2] relieved our brigade in order to give us three nights' rest, our physical strength being so much reduced. Nötting and self slept together in the same tent.

The whole Battalion went to bed very early. I undressed for the first time in seven weeks and had sank into a sound repose. About two o'clock this morning Captain Nötting cried out, 'Wheatley, Wheatley, don't you hear?' I listened and said, 'Only the outposts skirmishing,' and fell asleep instantly. Nötting again awoke me with, 'I'm sure the French are coming out. Hark!' I heard a pop, then another. All was silent again, and I was on the point of again falling off, when more than five hundred reports burst upon our ears, a thunder of cannon followed, and loud cries of 'Fall in!' Fall in!' echoed over the hills and heaths.

[While Sir John Hope's force had been engaged on the tedious blockade of Bayonne, endeavouring, as Wheatley puts it, to starve out the infernal fortress, the rest of Wellington's army had been driving the French back

---

1. *King Henry IV*, Part I, iii, 201.
2. Robinson's brigade in the 5th Division – the 2nd Battalion of the 47th, 1st/4th and 2nd/59th.

towards the Garonne. First at Orthez on the Gave du Pau at the end of February, then at Aire at the beginning of March, Soult's disintegrating army was defeated and pushed back to the north-east. On 12 March, Beresford, detached with a small, fast-moving force, entred Bordeaux; and on 11 April, after a last desperate resistance, Soult evacuated Toulouse.

Napoleon had already abdicated, and the long war was over. Yet at Bayonne, Thouvenot refused to give way.

It had been Wellington's intention that the town should be formally besieged, but Hope had carried his siege operations forward slowly, believing wrongly that the garrison of 14,000 men had little food and could be starved into surrender. And so when news arrived on 10 April that the Allies had entered Paris and the Emperor had been deposed, Hope's men were still waiting disconsolately for the garrison to lay down their arms. The news from the north reached the garrison both by means of letters smuggled into the town and by messages shouted across the lines. It drove Thouvenot to fury, and in a gesture of despairing rage he threw out his garrison into an assault on his besiegers at St Etienne, an assault which could achieve nothing but the waste of death.]

The repeated flashes of the cannon from Bayonne and the shells in the air enabled us to find our clothes and in five minutes the whole Brigade was on its way. Nothing could equal the beauty of the scene. The stillness of night doubled the report of the ordnance. The air filled with stars and shells like a Vauxhall exhibition; and the very earth appeared like a mirror reflecting the lights of the atmosphere, for every bush and hedge was spangled with flashing stars from the musketry, and the fields covered with blue lights shot from Bayonne to shew the men on the ramparts when our troops passed where to direct their guns.

An immense bomb hovered over our heads and in the act of falling scattered our battalion over a large field. But men are like sheep. A common danger attracts them; and they soon returned to a body, the Officers being the nucleus of attraction.

The little I have read of gunnery has informed me never to avoid a shell in the air and I cannot persuade my brother Officers to imitate me. Llewellyn and myself on this occasion put it into practice; for I ran to meet it, by which means you avoid it as is generally the case in all apparent danger.

If [I am standing] at (a) and I look at the shell (b), by running at it I shall be at (c) when the bomb drops at (d).

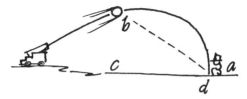

On getting into the heat of the fight I found the warfare an unpleasant one, as not a soul could be seen. Now and then a voice in the hedge would say 'Français ou Anglais?' and a thrust through the bush was an answer. Our Brigade Major, Dreschel, lost his life that way. The same Question was put to him and instead of jumping into it, he proudly answered, 'A German,' when a ball in his groin convinced him how much the snake in the bush respected his nativity. Giesmann[1] and Buhse[2] seized the Frenchman and sent him in the rere, an honorable prisoner. Lord Ellenborough[3] would have acted otherwise. What incongruity!

Our Battalion now drew up in a small garden. The French were around us and it was impossible to distinguish Friends from foes. The French had seized the Windmill in our rere and we began to fear for our Camp and baggage. The batteries played increasingly, and the wounded lay very numerous around. It was impossible to send them in the rere as no hospital had been appointed. By the flashes of light I saw something wrapped in a boat cloak on the other side of the hedge.

Impelled by curiosity as well as humanity, I broke through and on turning it up I washed away the blood and gore from the features with the skirt of the wrapper and discovered the countenance of Lieutenant Köhler of my Regiment. My promotion instantly suggested itself and thoughts of my own danger. I walked up to Captain Bacmeister and, bowing, said in the midst of the shot, 'Allow me to introduce Lieutenant E. Wheatley to your notice.' And I actually received his congratulation. Can there be any thirst for glory when actions like these take

1. Ensign Louis Giesmann, 5th Line Battalion K.G.L.
2. Lieutenant George Buhse, 5th Line Battalion K.G.L.
3. Edward Law, First Baron Ellenborough (1750–1818). In 1802 he had succeeded Lord Kenyon as Chief Justice of the King's Bench and was renowned not only for his profound legal knowledge but for his stern and domineering manner to counsel and to prisoners in the dock.

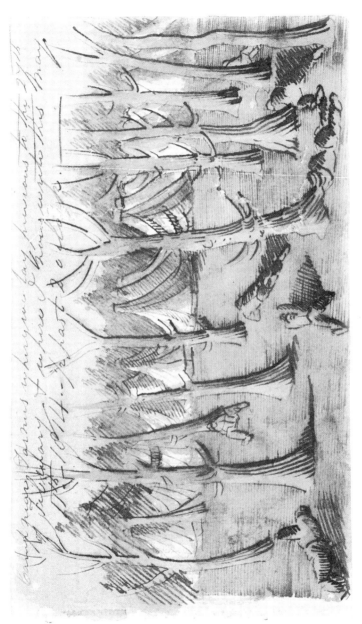

Plate 13 'Returned to our old camp near Tarnos.'

Plate 14a 'Labouheyre Girls wear the following mode.'

Plate 14b 'Two blankets thrown over a stick was our house.'

place on the fields of havock? Ambition's made of sterner stuff. Interest is the impulse in these our modern wars. Paulus Emilius threw his spoils into the public treasury.[1] I throw mine into my private pocket.

Nothing could be more harrassing than our occupation till day break – firing at hazard, the men dropping, killed by an invisible adversary.

In the warmth of a volley of small arms a ball came through the hedge, tore off the fourth button on my right breast, went through Nötting's arm and severely wounded Bacmeister in the knee. He fell. Nötting, in his fear, begged of me to keep from him as no luck ensued where I was, and I'm sure no good results from his society. Nor do I know who ever is benefitted by it.

As soon as day light appeared, a little amusement began. We drove the French back with the bayonet, scoured the fields, gave three huzzas and stood behind the stone walls from the cannon shot. While engaged firing over these places, I was surprised [by] something heavily falling in the earth without noise. So watching the next fall, I went up to the spot and turning up the earth with my sword discovered a cannon ball within. Astonished, I fancied the very clouds [were] firing upon us; so, telling Llewellyn, we watched and at last discovered that the French, to save shells, fired their shot perpendicularly in order to catch us in our hiding places.

About eight o'clock the French ceased firing and looking into the Town [I] discovered the three colored flag down and the white hoisted.

A solemn pause of half an hour ensued [and then] a sudden order to bury the dead came round.

[The confusion of the fighting which Wheatley describes was general throughout Hope's force. The K.G.L. were not taken by surprise, for a deserter had given warning of the intended assault and General Hinüber had taken the precaution of putting all his battalions under arms. Napier thought, however, that General James Hay, the Divisional Commander, disbelieved the deserter's story. Certainly he 'took no additional precautions: and it is probable that neither the German brigades nor the reserves of the

---

1. Paulus Lucius Aemilius (*c.* 229–160 B.C.), the Roman general entrusted with the command in the Macedonian War which he ended with his victory at Pydna in 168 B.C. Macedonia became a Roman province, and although he had many opportunities to make a fortune from its riches he did not do so, and died a poor man.

Guards would have been put under arms but for the activity of Hinüber'.[1]
*In any event the power and abruptness of the attack on a moonless night
were alarming. General Hay was killed in its opening stages at the church
of St Etienne which was soon afterwards captured; and Sir John Hope,
who had already been criticized by Wellington after the battle of the Nive
for 'placing himself among the sharpshooters without (as they do) shelter-
ing himself from the enemy's fire',*[2] *was wounded and taken prisoner as he
dashed headlong towards the threatened area.*

*General Hinüber counterattacked on his own responsibility and it was
this action, combined with General Howard's independent counterattack
on the other flank, which saved the situation.*

*French and Allied losses were both heavy, the French having nearly
1,000 casualties and the Allies over 800, including 236 prisoners. The
Guards suffered most heavily. The K.G.L. losses were 189. Wheatley's
battalion lost two officers (Lieutenants Charles Köhler and Augustus
Meyer) and seven men were killed; and two officers (Captains Nötting
and Bacmeister) and eleven men were wounded.*

*'It is an odd circumstance, but I believe true,' wrote Larpent, 'that the
sort of notice we had of an intended sortie by the enemy at Bayonne, which
was given by a deserter just before it took place, only did us mischief. The
out pickets were doubled, and as no picket could stand the rush of four or
five thousand men, we only lost so many more prisoners by this.'*[3]

*'Altogether,' Fortescue concludes, 'this was a very bloody little combat
for there was much actual fighting with the bayonet – a rare occurrence –
and the bayonet is the deadliest of all weapons.'*[4]]

The French poured out from the town, unarmed, and a singular
scene ensued – they picking up their dead, and we ours. I went under
the French batteries and had a long chat with some French Officers
who gave me some snuff. And as the French soldiers passed us with
their dead comrades, we reflected on the miserable trade of war.

Suddenly a blank shot was fired from the Citadel. We hastily shook
hands and in five minutes I was as eager to shoot them as they had
been to present their *râpé* to me.

About half past nine we returned to Camp, triumphantly playing
our Regimental march in spite of their shot, and I now write this next
the tent wherein lie Meyer and Köhler smashed and lacerated. Last

1. Napier, *op. cit.*, vi, 172–3.
2. *Despatches*, xi, 372.
3. Larpent, *op. cit.*, iii, 200.
4. Hon. J. W. Fortescue, *A History of the British Army* (x), 97.

night they rejoiced over the social bowl. Tonight the voice of mirth and jollity is still to them for ever. Had we all the spirit of divination the prospect of inevitable destruction open to our view would embitter every worldly joy. The goodness of God is manifest in this point, and evidently testifies his omniscience as well as the beneficence of his dealings towards us in suffering our future happenings to depend upon our own gratitude and actions towards him.

2 May   Peace concluded.

*

9 May   Returned to our old Camp near Tarnos which we occupied previous to the battle of the 27th February [Plate 13, *facing p. 48*].

How long this tranquillity will exist I know not. My life is preserved and I now do not despair of again seeing Old England. I have been a little knocked about but my limbs and senses are entire, thank God. And I am promoted. As my privations have been severe I shall enjoy my pleasures with more relish. I must always to be grateful for my preservation. I shall now correspond at home and no more to myself.

If the reading of this journal, written abroad in all weathers and at short and long intervals, will convey as much amusement or rather entertainment to Eliza Brookes as the writing it was satisfactory to Edmund Wheatley, I shall feel content indeed with the thought that hours and hours of pastime may be productive of one moment's amusement to my ever inestimable Eliza. And could I prolong that moment to years, the proportionate time required on my part would appear as short as have many of those delightful walks I have taken with her who is my strongest hope and my only fortune in this world.

With the aid of memory I shall as short as possible write my last Campaign until my disbandment.

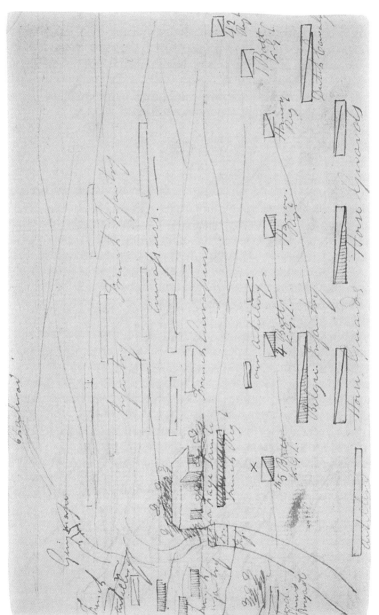

Fig. 4 Wheatley's sketch of Waterloo

PART TWO

The Waterloo Campaign, 1815

[In June 1814 the 1st Division struck camp at Le Boucau and marched north for Bordeaux on the first stage of its journey back to England.]

21 June 1814   Left our Camp at Tarnos near Bayonne and marched to St Vincent.

22 June   Castets. In a deep wood.

23 June   Slept in a barn with Nötting. In the cool of the evening, wishing to ride over an immense heath to see its extent, I mounted an immense fiery jack Ass without bridle or saddle, and by the aid of a stick had guided him about a mile and a half, when suddenly turning round, he made for home with the most unruly anticks. I kept my seat for some time. At length he gave such a twist with his head and hind legs that he fetched me clean over him on the side of my head amidst the laughter of Nötting and the Grenadier Company.

24 June   To Labouheyre. Slept in a ditch with Llewellyn. Every village between Bayonne and Bordeaux [is] remarkable for a difference of fashion. Labouheyre Girls wear the following mode, all alike *[Plate 14a, facing p. 49]*.

We marched through a small village yesterday where the men, women and children all walked upon stilts, and nothing could equal the originality of the scene where crowds of human beings seemed elevated in a supernatural manner. Some walked three or four miles with us, performing feats of dexterity.

25 June   Marched through a burning forest.

26 June   Four miles from Bordeaux.

27 June   Marched through Bordeaux [with] musick playing and colors flying. This city is called le petit Paris and it is not undeserving of the name. The Garonne flows on its side and is filled with trading vessels from all countries. La rue du chapeau rouge is far superior to Oxford Street; and the external architecture of the Theatre is magnificent in the extreme. Every necessary of life is dogcheap and the people civil and kind. After a tedious march through it, we encamped on an immense heath three miles distant from the City called Blanquefort, where we once more joined the whole British Army.

8 *July* [Still] waiting for orders to march to a place of embarkation for Old England.

At Blanquefort heath the tents were sent to the stores and we were obliged to shift as we could. The army having received three months [pay] out of nine due to us, my employment was dissipation and my idea schemes of amusement. The Theatre I attended regularly and discovered the Gascon ladies not inferior to the Parisians in vivacité. Respectable girls sometimes dress themselves as men, and three or four, arm in arm, would lounge in the evening along the Promenade with all the airs of our Bond Street petit maîtres, then, giggling when they met anyone, run as if to entice a pursuit. This is gaieté!!!

From this encampment I wrote to all my friends in England and countermanded one directed to Wallingford. I will endeavour to represent the mansion in which this packet was made to shew the life of a soldier and what he is accustomed to. Two blankets thrown over a stick was our house on account of the tents being restored [Plate 14b, *facing p. 49*]. But wine or good claret was 3d a bottle, so all is proportion.

9 *July* Left Blanquefort and Bordeaux and after three days pleasant marching reached the mouth of the Garonne [*Gironde*] at a small sea port called Pauillac. Here we sold our cattle, as cheap as mud. My gigantic jackey [*jackass*] I parted with for five dollars and he stood me in fifty seven.

7 *August* On the shore our amusements were bathing, drinking and sleeping, lounging about the coffee house, billiards, etc.

14 *August* Embarked on board the Alfred Transport.

19 *August* Moved to the Egmont, a Battleship. Fine weather. Heart

light, as [whose] would not be when the prospect of once more visiting ones natal spot is in view.

20 August   Arrived in Portsmouth harbour after a pleasant voyage. Strange it was I should return the very day I left it twelve months back.

30 August   Disembarked and marched to Chichester.

31 August   Marched to Arundel Barracks. Here I endeavoured to procure leave of absence but could not succeed, an order was against it. So early in the morning I took post-chaise and ran off to Brighton [where] I launched out into dissipation to drown the reflection of a disappointment so cruel to the feelings of one whose most sanguine desire was to revisit his friends and receive their congratulation.

4 September   Left Brighton for Worthing, Southampton, etc., and joined my Regiment at Hastings. Put in arrest. Here I again exerted myself to go to London but we expected to march daily.

[*After the peace all the non-German troops in the K.G.L. were discharged and the Legion took on a more national character. The British officers, however, retained their commissions, and Wheatley was annoyed that after only a few days in England, during which he saw neither his brother nor Eliza Brookes, he was to be sent back to the Continent for garrison duty.*]

6 September   Marched to Canterbury, Ashford and entered quarters in Barracks.

9 September   Marched to Ramsgate and embarked on board a dirty Transport.

10 September   Sailed from Ramsgate at Sunset, the pier being lined with Ladies and Gentlemen, who gave us three cheers. This return to England was the most tantalizing to my feelings and none but myself can suppose the poignancy of feeling I endured as the vessel reeled out of harbour and as the shore imperceptibly diminished to a vapour in appearance.

11 September   Next morning we enter the dangerous harbor of Ostend. The shore lies so flat that you do not perceive the country until you actually are in it. The sandy hills appearing among the waves resembles them in color so much that the eye is completely deceived. Ostend is a dirty unwholesome place and the whole city is fortified pretty strongly. Buonaparte took down eight hundred houses to finish the fortifications.[1]

13 September   Disembarked and marched about three miles along the Escaut when we entered some large barges and had a most delightful ride until sunset when we reached Bruges, where we slept. Illuminations in the town, the King of Holland[2] being there.

14 September   Entered barges in the morning and after gliding in the Carthaginian style between flowery meads and smiling lawns (as poets sing) we arrived at night in Ghent.

15 September   Stopped behind with Knight[3] to visit the curiosities and reached the Regiment in a fiacre at Deyzne, three leagues onward, where I entered quarters at Mrs Steyverts, a tobacco shop. I had not been three days here before I discovered a keepsake the Captain of the English Transport had presented me with on leaving his vessel, for finding myself spotted like a rasin pudding I sent for Gerson to inform [him] I imagined the Scarlet fever had seized hold of me. But he quickly undeceived my conjecture. Sending [for] a couple of men, they stripped me naked and covered me with a mud composition all over. I looked like the Venus di Medicis when it's transported from one country to another. And it was only on my recovery I learnt I had been amused with the Scotch fiddle,[4] for the Ship blankets contained a most virulent itch and I had unfortunately hugged them too affectionately.

We remained at Deynze until the 18th of October and I must acknowledge I led a very pleasant life while my thoughts were con-

1. Wheatley's movements from landing at Ostend, until his arrival at Mons in June 1815, are shown in a map on p. 92.
2. William I (1772–1844). When Holland rose in revolt against French domination in 1813, William, who had fought bravely against Napoleon, landed at Scheveningen after eighteen years' exile and was proclaimed Prince Sovereign of the Netherlands. He assumed the title of King in 1814. His son, the Prince of Orange, born in 1792, was on Wellington's staff in the Peninsular War and is mentioned later in Wheatley's Diary.
3. Henry Knight, the battalion's Paymaster.
4. Also the Welsh fiddle, slang for itch – *O.E.D.*

fined to the Country. Regimental balls to the adjacent Gentry and nobility formed our principal pastimes. Here I began musick playing for the first time, and great regret was unfeignedly expressed by the inhabitants when we left the place which took place on the 19th when we marched to Oudenaarde, a large dirty place celebrated for the Victory gained by the Duke of Marlborough in Queen Anne's time.

20 October   Slept in a miserable garret without furniture in a house on a common.

20 October   After a wet, windy, cold, dreary march, about five o'clock we entered in a shower of rain into Tournai. I took up my lodging at No. 5, la rue des Carmis, at Mrs Crepins, a Baker's widow, and soon became initiated into the mysteries as well as revelries of the City.

The City of Tournai is one of the most ancient fortresses in the Low Countries. Many vestiges of Antiquity are still visible in the place. The Escaut runs through it. The Citadel was Vauban's[1] masterpiece and was impregnable. Louis XVI, after the battle of Fontenoy, blew it up; and the ruins still bespeak its pristine might. General Morison bombarded it a short time; and the Church near the Port de Lille is perforated with cannonshot.

Tournai has one Theatre, somewhat larger than our Country playhouses such as Richmond, Bexhill, etc. And the performers, being of the itinerant class, there are no stated seasons for performing. Weekly public balls were in vogue while I was there, and they were well attended. In these assemblies connections are formed; but the greatest animosity exists between the Nobility and the tradespeople, and it requires the nicest discrimination of deportment to preserve the good opinion and acquaintance of the two Classes.

It would be tedious to my fair reader were I to enter into a detail of the several amusements, laws and customs of this place, suffice to say the months I spent there were the most pleasing, the most instructive and the most amusing of any I ever enjoyed when absent from her. The numerous acquaintances I formed and the endeavours they made to render my hours agreeable and satisfactory will never be recalled without esteem and gratitude.

Here is a rough sketch of Tournai as taken one morning when on a

1. Sébastien le Prestre de Vauban (1633–1707), Marshal of France, and the greatest military engineer of his time.

working party at the Citadel on the Esplanade. The town is surrounded with a brick wall and when the French scaled the outward ramparts the Prussians made a stout resistance from the interior of the Gardens. The inhabitants still preserve several balls shining in their garden enclosures. The Cathedral [*in the background*] is an ancient gigantick building[1] [Plate 16, *facing p. 65*]. The interior has naught remarkable.

1 March Still at Tournai.

2 April While dressing to go out to a party, the girl came in pale and aghast telling me the cannon was planted 'sur la grande place' with lighted matches, and that Boney was at Lille.

[*Napoleon, after his escape from Elba, had arrived at Lyons on 10 March and announced that he had come to save France. Numerous units of the Bourbon army had gone out to prevent his advance on Paris, but had greeted him instead with shouts of admiration and protestations of loyalty to death. On 14 March he was joined by Marshal Ney and on the night of 20 March he was sleeping at the Tuileries.*

The Allies at Vienna ordered an immediate mobilization of their armies and appointed the Duke of Wellington to the command of the troops already in the Low Countries.]

A sudden order came instantly to run to the Citadel and take the Guard there.

3 April On guard or on piquet at the different gates at Tournai.

8 April A multitude of reports prevalent. Fresh regiments pour'd in daily and the Garrison soon became treble in strength.

9 April Left Tournai, through Ath to a small dirty village with seven houses. Six officers in one room. We remained in this unsociable spot as in a wilderness until the 16th when we marched to a comfortable quarter and dined at the Mayor of Brussels's Chateau every day.

6 May Marched into [a] Monastery with magnificent Gardens,

1. The Cathedral of Notre Dame, one of the finest Romanesque and Gothic buildings in Belgium. Its foundation dates from 1030, though it was mainly built in the thirteenth and fourteenth centuries.

and amused myself with fishing and walking. In short became quite rusticated.

11 May Through Soignies to Naast.

31 May At Naast. Pleasant time. Quite in the Country. My ideas became rural and had my genius been poetic, my strains would have been pastoral!!!

14 June Still at Naast. Amusements meditative and contemplative. Here My English Correspondents became regular. I suppose they felt interested in the expected Campaign and expected my dispatches.

15 June Marched through Braine-le-Comte to Marche-lez-Ecaussines, a pretty town.

16 June Bivouacked in a field. Heard dreadful cannonading near Fleurus. While in this field and knowing the almost certainty of an approaching battle, I endeavoured to stir up the spirit of Captain Nötting in order to revenge myself. But great talkers are little doers.

[*The day before, 15 June, Napoleon with 124,000 men had struck at the Allied forces concentrating behind the Sambre and had driven his columns between the right of Field-Marshal von Blücher's 113,000 Prussians and the 83,000 troops of various nationalities under Wellington's command. On 16 June, while Wheatley on his way to the front from Marche-lez-Ecaussines was listening to the 'dreadful cannonading' near Fleurus, Napoleon was defeating Blücher at Ligny and Wellington was striving to hold back Ney at Quatre Bras.*

Soon the French were to advance on Brussels; but not as they had hoped between the divided Allied armies. For Blücher had retreated north to Wavre on a line parallel to Wellington's troops, who were making for a ridge which crossed the Brussels – Charleroi road a mile and a half south of the village of Waterloo.]

The cannonading was very loud and frequent all the afternoon. A thick wood at a distance was envelop'd in smoke, and at intervals a strong flash of light could be caught in the dusky hue at a distance. The sound was at times close, sometimes receded – so uncertain is war. The suspense and anxiety of our situation was indescribable, for none but those who have experienced the uneasiness of mind a soldier endures when standing for orders to move in sound of battle, can conceive the astonishing length to which the moments are stretched on so critical an occasion. Just at sunset we were put on the move and every noise was hushed. We marched nearly three hours unknowing our destination, until three or four wounded passing convinced us that every step was bringing us nearer and nearer to the scene of slaughter. The crowd of mutilated, lacerated objects soon increased which I only discovered by their cries and groans as they passed. At length we arrived on a wide plain. The road more elevated. Broken muskets, soldiers caps and shoes were strewed on the road; and on each side were numerous blankets stretched out, under which lay the pining, forsaken wounded soldiers. A strong melancholy seized me as I marched by these moaning heaps of bruised valour. At times I could perceive by the starlight a feeble motion in the white coverings; and a painful scream would accompany the attempt to ease the shattered limb. A few hours [ago] they were enjoying low jokes and converse. One small moment has produced more contrition in the heart than ten thousand pathetic admonitions could effect. And the feverish tongue now pronounced 'My God!' which days before prophaned the sacred word in the utterance.

At length a distant humming with lights bespoke our approach to the main body. And in the course of two hours we were stationed behind a high hedge. On piquet all night.

17 June About break of day a high wind arose which quickly brought rains. And about two o'clock the grenadier Company was ordered to head-quarters where the Quarter Master General ordered us to clear the high road of all carts and carriages as far as Brussels and to suffer nothing but Artillery to come up. Captain Nötting ordered me to leave him with thirteen men [*and to clear the roads*] at Genappe and then to join the Company at Brussels at night, which I had resolved not to do before he desired me, as I was confident a grand battle would take place and I had never been absent in the least skirmish since I first campaign'd.

At Genappe I found sufficient employment for my whole Regiment. The town was choked up with wounded, and crowds and crowds of cavalry poured in [*from Quatre Bras*] each man leading his horse by the bridle with a wounded foot soldier laying across the saddle. A thought instantly suggested itself that instead of driving off the Commissary carts of beef and liquor, I would empty them in the ditches and put the wounded in them, which my men succeeded in [doing] with considerable opposition. I had seized a covered waggon belonging to the train of the Duke of Brunswick[1] and was assisting some wounded Belgians in when the Brunswick Serjeant of the escort gallop'd up, and had I not parried with my sword [he] would have laid my skull open. The fellow instantly perceived my wings and before I could return the Compliment was out of sight.

In the course of two hours we had pretty well cleared the place.

When [I was] turning out of a street up came Commissary Beverly, followed by half a dozen waggons of beef and biscuit. I stood up to my knee in mud just then and was bellowing out some order, when, knowing my voice, he gallop'd up on his fiery horse. 'Oh, Wheatley. How are ye? What think you of this mare? 150 guinea touch.'

'I'll trouble you to move your Regiment as soon as possible,' I answered. 'I'll examine your mare at a more convenient season.'

He trotted off instantly and I sent his Brigade after him.

What provoked [me] was his prancing the mud in my face, by which manoeuvre my military hat fell in the mud, out of which dropped my night Cap and some brown bread which were completely soaked.

I then collected my men and marched [through] Nivelles [to] Mont St Jean. At this latter place I halted the detachment and went into a house to procure some water. The place was filled with soldiers of all nations; but entering a small dark bedroom I pulled back the window curtain and rested myself. As I leaned on the table I fancied I heard a noise in the bed. Pulling open the curtain I saw a man lying in his clothes. I enquired who he was when a feeble voice begged of me in french for some water. After drinking it he told me he was a Dutch officer, that he had been wounded the day previous in the ribs by a ball and had had no surgical attendance. Having none to give him, I put into his hand one franc and some sous, all I had to purchase him some little requisite. Then marched further on with my men.

About half past four or five o'clock, I rested them in a ditch, it was so hot. But three or four [of them] went away and returned soon with a tub of small beer [which] they knocked on the head; and although I disapproved of the art, my thirst quenched the impulse of my conscience and the beverage quenched the fever of my drought.

About night we reached a large wood on the right [of the] road to Brussels, where we again rested.

1. Friedrich Wilhelm, Duke of Brunswick (1771–1815), brother of the Prince Regent's wife Caroline, had been killed at Quatre Bras the day before.

The Duke of Wellington rode by just then, and sent an aid de Camp into the place to enquire my business there, which I stated, and he rode on. When he was out of sight I broke open a barn where we all slept, confident of a battle next morning. When the men were all on the straw – after, poor fellows, they had made me [a bed from] the cleanest – I stated my determination to return next morning to the Army, and if any chose to join Nötting at Brussels they might, to which proposition none assented.

Before daybreak I aroused them. Poor fellows! The last time! And came up to the Division about five o'clock. [They] enquired after Nötting and why I was there, to which questions I stated all facts.

[Wellington's troops were now establishing themselves on the ridge south of Brussels where he had chosen to block Napoleon's path. Until Blücher joined him from the east, Wellington knew that he could expect to do no more than stand his ground in a position which made it possible to act offensively when the opportunity offered. Of the 63,000 troops under his command only the 21,000 British regulars and the 5,500 men of the King's German Legion were men in whose fighting ability he felt confident. These men, therefore, he had decided to place at the points of greatest danger.

Since two of Blücher's corps could be expected to arrive on his left flank during the course of the day, he was more concerned for the safety of his right, particularly so as Napoleon might be expected to incline in that direction to strike towards Brussels without the fear of entanglement with any Prussian troops which might be advancing from the east. Also the lower ground on Wellington's right flank around Hougoumont, where the French might move unseen around the west shoulder of the plateau, favoured an attack on that side. Here, therefore, he placed two of his British divisions, one of which included two brigades of the K.G.L. On their left, in the centre of his position where the Genappe–Brussels road crossed over the ridge south of the village of Mont St Jean, he placed others of his trusted troops. These included Lieutenant-General Karl Alten's 3rd Division; and it was in this Division that the 5th Line Battalion K.G.L. (which Wheatley had rejoined contrary to Captain Nötting's orders) was now serving.

The battalion was no longer commanded by Baron Ompteda, who had been given the brigade, but by Lieutenant-Colonel William, Baron Linsingen, formerly of the 6th Battalion.

Baron Linsingen was ordered to take up a position to the left of the Brussels road about half a mile south of Mont St Jean in the position indicated by the rectangle in the plan on page 90. In front of them, about

100 yards down the southern slope of the hill was a farm known as La Haye Sainte. And here the 2nd Light Battalion, commanded by Major George Baring, was placed amongst the skirmishers.

This part of the front was under the general direction of the 22-year-old Prince of Orange.]

18 June Nothing could exceed the miserable state in which I found the army in the morning. The rain had poured down in torrents all night, and that so powerfully as to preclude all possibility of kindling a fire. The army had fallen back considerably and I found my Battalion on the right of the high road near Mont St Jean. The whole Division was ranged in line on the most eminent part of the plain which shelved down gradually and then rose as progressively.

In the hollow was the scene of action and on the opposite heights we could perceive large dark moving masses of something impossible to distinguish individually. Where the edge of the ground bound the horizon, shoals of these gloomy bodies glided down, disjointing then contracting, like fields of animated clods sweeping over the plains, like melted lava from a Volcano, boding ruin and destruction to whatever dared impede its course. It had a fairy look and border'd on the supernatural in appearance. While gazing with all my utmost stretch of vision on the scene, little Gerson struck me on the shoulder saying, 'That's a battle, my boy! That's something like a preparation! You'd better have stopped with Nötting at Brussels. I must be off to the Hospital and I hope to see you there.'

We shook hands and I walked up and down for some time and felt very uneasy that I had left no letter of remembrance behind me.

I fancied the occupation of all at home. It was about six o'clock. Just then (a cloudy drizzly morning) my brother, I thought, was unconcernedly packing up orders or reading calmly some new publication. I concluded you, my Dearest Eliza, you, whom I always regreted, I was certain was asleep innocent and placid. The pillow that supported you was unconscious of its lovely burthen. But the breast, then cold and chilled with the prospect of approaching dissolution, felt that morning one or two warm sensations. It is an awful situation to be in, to stand with a sharp edged instrument at one's side, waiting for the signal to drag it out of its peaceful innocent house to snap the thread of existence of those we never saw, never spoke to, never offended.

On the opposite ascent stand hundreds of young men like myself whose feelings are probably more acute, whose principles are more upright, whose acquaintance would delight and conversation improve me, yet with all my soul I wished them dead as the earth they tramped on and anticipated their total annihilation. 'Tis inconceptible how one's ideas should be so diametrically reversed from what is equitable and correct. When I looked at my own comrades I could not conceive why my animosity was diverted from them in preference to the French who are, by far, more commendable characters than these heavy, selfish Germans.

Here stood a swelled-faced, ignorant booby, raw from England, staring with haggard and pallid cheek on the swarms of foes over against him. One could perceive the torture of his feelings by the hectic quivering of his muscles, as if fear and cold were contending for the natural color of the cheek. And this man is one of the mighty warriors shortly to deal out thunder and confusion to the opposers of the British constitution.

Close behind him stalked a dark, swarthy weather-beaten man, whose arm had aided in expelling the opposite nation from the Tagus to the Garonne. Frequent flashes from the pan had dyed his brows with a never-failing black. The horrid preparations before him gave no surprise to his soul. The scene afforded no novelty to his eye. Yet a side glance on turning at his walk's end bespoke the uppermost thoughts in his mind, [for] the oldest veteran must have been struck with the solemnity of the scene.

About ten o'clock, the order came to clean out the muskets and fresh load them. Half an allowance of rum was then issued, and we descended into the plain, and took our position in solid Squares. When this was arranged as per order, we were ordered to remain in our position but, if we like, to lay down, which the battalion did [as well as] the officers in the rere.

I took this opportunity of surveying our situation. It was singular to perceive the shoals of Cavalry and artillery suddenly in our rere all arranged in excellent order as if by a magic wand. The whole of the horse Guards stood behind us. For my part I thought they were at Knightsbridge barracks or prancing on St James's Street.

A Ball whizzed in the air. Up we started simultaneously. I looked at my watch. It was just eleven o'clock, Sunday (Eliza just in Church at Wallingford or at Abingdon) morning. In five minutes a stunning noise took place and a shocking havock commenced.

Plate 15 'Skulking like an outlaw in a thicket.'

Plate 16 'The Cathedral is an ancient gigantick building.'

[The battle began at about half past eleven with a French attack on the position at Hougoumont. Napoleon had, however, decided to wait until one o'clock, when the ground would be drier and his artillery consequently more dangerous, before opening his main attack on the Allied centre.

'As the rain fell in streams,' the 5th Line Battalion's journal records, 'the armies remained quiet till midday, and our cooking proceeded. Reconnaissances were carried out on both sides, and we could distinguish Napoleon on his grey horse.'

It was, in fact, nearer one o'clock than eleven that Napoleon – although he had already seen the unexpected approach of the Prussians on his right – launched on the Allied centre the appalling bombardment which Wheatley describes.]

One could almost feel the undulation of the air from the multitude of cannon shot. The first man who fell was five files on my left. With the utmost distortion of feature he lay on his side and shrivelling up every muscle of the body he twirled his elbow round and round in acute agony, then dropped lifeless, dying as it's called a death of glory, heaving his last breath on the field of fame. *Dieu m'engarde!*

A black consolidated body was soon seen approaching and we distinguished by sudden flashes of light from the sun's rays, the iron-cased cavalry of the enemy. Shouts of 'Stand firm!' 'Stand fast!' were heard from the little squares around and very quickly these gigantic fellows were upon us.

No words can convey the sensation we felt on seeing these heavy-armed bodies advancing at full gallop against us, flourishing their sabres in the air, striking their armour with the handles, the sun, gleaming on the steel. The long horse hair, dishevelled by the wind, bore an appearance confounding the senses to an astonishing disorder. But we dashed them back as cooly as the sturdy rock repels the ocean's foam. The sharp-toothed bayonet bit many an adventrous fool, and on all sides we presented our bristly points like the peevish porcupines assailed by clamorous dogs.

The horse Guards[1] then came up and drove them back; and

1. The Blues formed part of the Household Brigade under Lord Edward Somerset, the elder brother of Lord FitzRoy Somerset (the future Lord Raglan) who was serving as the Duke of Wellington's principal A.D.C. Other regiments in the Brigade were the 1st and 2nd Life Guards and the 1st Dragoon Guards. The Brigade was led in this charge by Lord Uxbridge, the Cavalry Commander, personally. A good account is contained in *One-Leg: The Life and Letters of Henry William Paget, 1768-1854* by the Marquess of Anglesey (Cape, 1961). See also Edith Saunders, *The Hundred Days* (Longmans, 1964), *The Hundred Days*, edited by Antony Brett-James (Macmillan, 1964) and Bryant, *op. cit.*

although the sight is shocking 'tis beautiful to see the skirmish of Cavalry.

The French made repeated attacks of this kind. But we stood firm as the ground we stood on, and two long hours were employed in these successive attacks.

About two o'clock the cavalry ceased annoying and the warfare took a new turn. In order to destroy our squares, the enemy filled the air with shells, howitzers and bombs, so that every five or six minutes, the whole Battalion lay on its face then sprang up again when [the danger] was over.

The Prince of Orange gallop'd by, screaming out like a new born infant, 'Form into line! Form into line!' And we obeyed.

About this time the battle grew faint and a mutual cannonade with musketry amused us for one and a half hours, during which time I walked up and down chatting and joking with the young officers who had not [until] then smelt powder.

An ammunition cart blew up near us, smashing men and horses. I took a calm survey of the field around and felt shocked at the sight of broken armour, lifeless bodies, murdered horses, shattered wheels, caps, helmets, swords, muskets, pistols, still and silent. Here and there a frightened horse would rush across the plain trampling on the dying and the dead. Three or four poor wounded animals standing on three legs, the other dangling before [them]. We killed several of these unfortunate beasts and it would have been an equal Charity to have perform'd the same operation on the wriggling, feverish, mortally lacerated soldiers as they rolled on the ground.

About four o'clock the battle was renewed with uncommon ardour. We still stood in line. The carnage was frightful. The balls which missed us mowed down the Dutch behind us, and swept away many of the closely embattled Cavalry behind them.

I saw a cannon ball take away a Colonel of the Nassau Regiment so cleanly that the horse never moved from under him. While [I was] buisy in keeping the men firm in their ranks, closing up the vacuities as the balls swept off the men, inspecting the fallen to detect deception [or] subterfuge, a regiment of Cuirassiers darted like a thunderbolt among us. At the instant a squadron of horse Guards dashed up to our rescue. In the confusion of the moment I made [for] the Colors to defend them. And we succeeded with infinite difficulty in rallying the men again.

I parried with great good fortune a back stroke from a horseman as he flew by me and Captain Sander[1] had a deep slice from the same fellow on the head the instant after.

The battalion once more formed into a solid square, in which we remained the [whole] afternoon.

I felt the ardor of the fight increase very much within me, from the uncommon fury of the engagement.

Just then I fired a slain soldier's musket until my shoulder was nearly jellied and my mouth was begrimed with gunpowder to such a degree that I champed the gritty composition unknowingly.

Nothing could equal the splendor and terror of the scene. Charge after charge succeeded in constant succession. The clashing of swords, the clattering of musketry, the hissing of balls, and shouts and clamours produced a sound, jarring and confounding the senses, as if hell and the Devil were in evil contention.

About this time I saw the Duke of Wellington running from a charge of Cavalry towards the Horse-Guards, waving his hat to beckon them to the encounter.

All our artillery in front fell into the french power, the bombardiers skulking under the carriages. But five minutes put them again into our hands and the men creeping out applied the match and sent confusion and dismay into the retreating enemy.

Several times were these charges renewed and as often defeated. Charge met charge and all was pellmell. The rays of the sun glittered on the clashing swords as the two opposing bodies closed in fearful combat and our balls clattered on the shining breastplates like a hail shower.

As I stood in the square I looked down, I recollect, to take a pinch of snuff and thought of the old ballad, which I had seen somewhere, of the aged Nurse who describes the glorious battles of Marlborough to the child. After each relation of valor and victory, the infant [says]

'Ten thousand slain you say and more?
What did they kill each other for?'
'Indeed I cannot tell', said she,
'But 'twas a famous victory.'[2]

The field was now thickened with heaps of bodies and shattered instruments. Carcases of men and beasts lay promiscuously entwined.

1. Captain Frederick Sander, 5th Line Battalion K.G.L. He was wounded again later in the day.
2. A misquotation, apparently, from Robert Southey's *The Battle of Blenheim*. The old person describing the battle is the grandfather, Kaspar, not the nurse.

Aid-de-Camps scoured across with inconceivable velocity. All was hurry and indefatigable exertion. The small squares on our right kept up incessant firings and the fight was as obstinate as at the commencement.

The Duke of Wellington passed us twice, slowly and cooly.

No advantage as yet was discernible on either side. The French Cavalry were less annoying. Their brave, repeated assaults had cost them very dear.

About six o'clock a passe-parole ran down the line – not to be disheartened, as the Prussians were coming up to our left, which news we received with loud cheers. And on looking [to] the left I perceived at some distance a dark swarm moving out of a thick wood. In twenty minutes a fresh cannonading began as if in rere of the French and the battle raged with increased vehemence.

A French Regiment of Infantry before us opposite the Farm house called the holy hedge (La Haye Sainte) advanced considerably just then and poured a destructive fire into our Battalion.

[By six o'clock Napoleon's position was extremely perilous. The Prussians were coming up on to his right flank in increasing strength, while the Allied right and centre despite all the exhausting and costly attacks that had been made upon them were still holding firm. Napoleon knew that he must break through Wellington's line before nightfall, or he would not get through at all.

Up till now he had been content to leave the tactical direction of the battle to Ney. But the time had come, he felt, for his own active and personal intervention. Dispatching eight battalions of the Imperial Guard to reinforce a holding action and counterattack on his right, he gave Ney orders to deliver a determined assault on the Allied centre and capture the key position of La Haye Sainte, where the 2nd Light Battalion, though now almost without ammunition, were still holding out.

Ney went into the attack soon after six. Baring's cruelly depleted companies were thrown out of the farm, and a column of infantry came up the ridge towards Wheatley's battalion. General Alten sent orders to the Brigade Commander Baron Ompteda, to deploy the battalion into line and repel the attack. Before passing the order on to Colonel Linsingen, Ompteda protested that 'such a movement could not be made without a useless sacrifice of men, more particularly as a body of the enemy cavalry lay in wait on the other side of the ravine'.

The Prince of Orange, who by this time was close to hysteria, sent his aide-de-camp, Lord John Somerset,[1] to repeat Alten's order. Already that day Ompteda had nearly lost the 5th Battalion by obeying a similar command. An aide-de-camp had galloped up, and had called out from a distance, 'Fifth Battalion! Deploy and advance!'

Ompteda, whose horse had been shot under him, had been standing inside the square that the battalion had formed as a protection against the Cavalry assaults. He had walked towards the A.D.C. and had said to him politely, 'Would it not be advisable to advance in square, and not form line till close to the enemy's infantry?'

'God damn it!' the A.D.C. had shouted back. 'My order is to order you to deploy immediately.'

The command had then been obeyed, and as soon as the movement had been completed and the battalion had begun its advance, it was attacked, as Ompteda had known it would be, by large numbers of cavalry. The square had been re-formed only just in time.

Colonel Ompteda was, then, determined to resist an order which once more threatened the battalion's existence. He told Lord John Somerset that it could not be obeyed, as the Horse Guards who had formerly supported them had been ordered to the left wing and the French Cuirassiers would surely attack them as soon as the infantry deployed. Lord John rode off for confirmation of his instructions. But shortly afterwards the Prince of Orange himself arrived with General Alten. Alten repeated the order and Ompteda repeated his representation, but when he added, 'We ought in any case to be supported by cavalry', and pointed to the French Cuirassiers who could be seen regrouping in the hollow, the Prince of Orange insisted they were not French but Dutch cavalry. Even when the Prince was convinced that he was wrong about this, he insisted that the command must nevertheless be obeyed; and 'in a sharp, peremptory manner said, "I must still repeat my order to attack in line with the bayonet, and I will listen to no further arguments." Colonel Ompteda merely replied in a loud voice, "Then I will." '

He was mounted again now, having taken the horse that had belonged to the Adjutant, Captain Schuck, who had been killed, and he rode to the front of the battalion with drawn sword.

'Try and save my two nephews,' he said to Colonel Linsingen, and then he gave the order to form line.[2]]

1. Captain Lord John Somerset, 23rd Foot (Royal Welch Fusiliers), was the seventh son of the 5th Duke of Beaufort. Lord Edward Somerset and Lord FitzRoy Somerset were his brothers.

2. Journal of 5th Line Battalion K.G.L.; Beamish, *op. cit.*, ii; Ompteda, *op. cit.*, 308–11. For a good modern account of the battle as a whole see John Naylor, *Waterloo* (Batsford, 1960).

Colonel Ompteda ordered us instantly into line to charge, with a strong injunction to 'walk' forward, until he gave the word. When within sixty yards he cried 'Charge', we ran forward huzzaing. The trumpet sounded and no one but a soldier can describe the thrill one instantly feels in such an awful moment. At the bugle sound the French stood until we just reached them. I ran by Colonel Ompteda who cried out, 'That's right, Wheatley!'

I found myself in contact with a French officer but ere we could decide, he fell by an unknown hand. I then ran at a drummer, but he leaped over a ditch through a hedge in which he stuck fast. I heard a cry of, 'The Cavalry! The Cavalry!' But so eager was I that I did not mind it at the moment, and when on the eve of dragging the Frenchman back (his iron-bound hat having saved him from a Cut) I recollect no more. On recovering my senses, I look'd up and found myself, bareheaded, in a clay ditch with a violent head-ache. Close by me lay Colonel Ompteda on his back, his head stretched back with his mouth open, and a hole in his throat. A frenchman's arm across my leg.

[*The battalion had been cut to pieces by the cavalry which had thundered down upon their flank and rear, as Colonel Ompteda had foreseen.*

Baron Ompteda himself had led the charge.

'I saw that the French had their muskets pointed at the Colonel,' Captain Charles Berger of the 5th Battalion said afterwards, 'but they did not fire. The officers struck the men's barrels up with their swords. They seemed astonished at the extraordinary calm approach of the solitary horseman whose white plume showed him to be an officer of high rank. He soon reached the enemy's line of infantry before the garden hedge. He jumped in, and I clearly saw his sword strikes smite the shakos off. The nearest French officer looked on with admiration without attempting to check the attack.' Then Captain Berger saw the Colonel 'sink from his horse and vanish'.[1]

When his body was later discovered in the ditch where Wheatley had lain, it was still fully clothed but the pockets had been plundered. The singed rim of the bullet hole in the high collar, told how close to him his assailant had been.

The death of 'this gallant officer', Fortescue thought, was 'an immolation to the ignorance and self sufficiency of the Prince of Orange. The

---

1. Ompteda, *op. cit.*

Prince himself was presently forced by a wound to quit the field, and none too soon.'[1]

Private Wheeler of the 57th had decided the month before that the Prince was 'not the man for us'.[2]

Colonel Linsingen was one of the very few officers to survive that disastrous charge unhurt. His horse was wounded and fell, rolling over on top of him, and by the time he had struggled to his feet he saw that his battalion had been virtually wiped out. He grabbed Ompteda's two young nephews and pulled them back to the safety of a hollow. There were less than twenty other survivors.]

So confused was I that I did not remember I was on the field of Battle at the moment. Lifting up a little, I look'd over the edge of the ditch and saw the backs of a french Regiment and all the day's employment instantly suggested itself to my mind. Suddenly I distinguished some voices and heard one say '*En voici! En voici!*'

I lay down as dead, retaining my breath, and fancied I was shot in the back of my head. Presently a fellow cries, '*Voici un autre b.*' And a tug at my epaulette bespoke his commission. A thought struck me – he would turn me round to rifle my pockets. So starting up, I leaped up the ditch; but a swimming seized me and I was half on the ground when the fellow thrust his hand in my collar, grinning, '*Ou va's tu, chien?*' I begged of him to let me pick up my cap and he dragged me into the house.

The inside of La Haye Sainte I found completely destroyed, nothing but the rafters and props remaining. The floor, covered with mortar bricks and straw, was strewed with bodies of the German Infantry and French Tirailleurs. A Major in Green lay by the door. The carnage had been very great in this place.

I was taken over these bodies out of a door on the right, through a garden to the back of the house where I found several Officers and men standing. [They] instantly crowded round me. One of my wings was on and the other half off. My oil skin haversac [was] across my shoulder, and my cap fastened to my waist, by running my sash through the internal lining.

A multitude of questions was put to me by the men and Officers while I fastened on my Cap: '*Vous êtes Chef de Battalion, Monsieur?*'

1. Fortescue, *op. cit.*, X, 383.
2. *The Letters of Private Wheeler, 1809–1828*, edited with a foreword by Captain B. H. Liddell-Hart (The Windrush Press, 1993).

'*Non, Je suis Lieutenant des Grenadiers.*'
'*Mais vous portez deux epaulettes.*'
'*Je suis Grenadier, je vous dis!*'[1]
'*Non, Non,*' said a good-temper'd Officer, tapping me on the Shoulder, '*Je connais votre uniforme. Oui, oui. Quand vous autres Anglais sont prisonniers, vous êtes capables de passer pour autres que vous n'êtes. Si, si, etc., etc.*'

I begged for some water and asked the officer to tell me if my head was cut or what it was, and I could only conclude I had been stunned it being much swelled.

An Officer and four men were placed with me, they persisting in my promotion contrary to the desire of the Prince Regent. And I had not walked five yards before the Officer with me took my watch and disappeared with one of the men.

On walking across the field from this house toward the high road, I saw a Cuirassier on his face with outstretched arms soaking in his blood. I never saw so gigantic a figure. I'm confident his height was 6' 9". He reminded me as I passed of Goliath in ye Scriptures.

On reaching the high road I saw a foot soldier in a strange attitude. His head, his hands and knees, bent up to his chest, were forced into the mud and he looked like a frog thrusting itself into the slimy puddle. Shocking! Just here the cannonading from our Artillery was so warm that the mud and bushes were dashed about us frightfully; and I was in imminent danger of dying disgracefully in the midst of the enemy. My keeper at last said surlily, '*Il n'est pas necessaire de se laisser tuer*'; and pushed me into a ditch, jumping after me. I took this opportunity of tying my handkerchief round my head. Here the fellow turned my pockets inside out [and] found a penknife and memorandum book. My last farthing I had given to a wounded Belgic Officer in Mont St Jean some days before.

While this ruffian stood under the shelter of the ditch I look up and surveyed the battle minutely. I saw our Cavalry behaving gallantly and felt a national pride at sight of our little squares, enveloped in a slight mist, surrounded by innumerable Foes. The ground on which I had stood since the morning was bare and I felt a chill on supposing the whole of my Comrades had sank under the French sword.

1. As explained in an earlier footnote, all officers of grenadier companies wore a pair of metal wings on the shoulders instead of the single fringed epaulette worn on the right shoulder by officers of the battalion companies. Since field officers (majors and above) wore a pair of fringed epaulettes, the confusion of Wheatley's captors is understandable.

[Wheatley had been wounded at the crisis of the battle. All the other Allied leaders in the centre being killed or wounded, Wellington took personal control. He restored confidence, there, as he instilled it everywhere, and the 'nearest thing you ever saw in your life' was slowly transformed into his greatest victory.]

While thus amusing myself, my guard struck me on the arm with '*Allons! Marché!!*' And we ascended the road on each side of which stood crowds and crowds of infantry.

The road here appeared cut through a hill, and as I looked up I saw two young officers pointing at me. By their gestures I understood their talk. One of them took out a white handkerchief from his pocket and unrolling it pointed a pistol at me, while the other instantly seized his arm. I set him down as a younker [*youngster*] from School, with a pawnbroker's pocket pistol bought to kill sparrows on the cherry trees.

The roads and ditches were crammed with groaning wounded, and really I felt for them as if they were English for military hatred is never felt for the helpless but against the daring and the Capable.

On passing this defile we entered into Genappe where the day before I was free as air, carrying terror and dismay among beef carts and biscuit waggons, [but now] a poor, cast down, bruised captive, exposed to the insults and bravado of thousands of intoxicated, insolent enemies. I entered the town alongside of a foot soldier on horseback, his right leg [so] shattered at the knee that his leg hung down by one single piece of sinew, and my stomach sickened as it dangled backwards and forwards splashing his horse with gore and marrow. The fellow pale and aghast, chewing dry biscuit to allay his scorching thirst.

'*Voila, un français!*' said an officer to me, pointing at him as I passed, proud of the fellow's fortitude, not envious of his situation.

The town was filled with troops. Before a large wooden gate stood a body of Grenadiers in line – a fine Corps. The man with me endeavoured to take me through, but the Officer repelled me with inconceivable disdain.

On reaching the pump on the right hand, I begged for some water, and just as I had placed it to my lips, a ruffian thrust me back with his horse, bestowing a bitter curse upon me which produced a wrangle between him and an officer. So the guard ordered me on.

When half in the town a fellow looked earnestly at me and

trotting up, tore the handkerchief off my head in a most barbarous manner.

I was then conducted down a street on the right. Against the wall of a Garden I saw a foot soldier sitting with his head back and both his eyeballs hanging on his cheecks, a ball having entered the side of his head and passed out at the other. Nothing could equal the horror of his situation. His mouth was open, stiff and clotted, clear blood oozed out of his ears and the purulent matter from his empty sockets emitted a pale stream from the vital heat opposed to the evening cold.

So much for honor! thought I. Will it replace his orbs? No. As Falstaff says, 'Who was it? He that died yesterday? No!! 'Tis a word coined by an apprentice over his sparkling glass', and the Morning Advertiser!

I was then conducted into an enclosed garden and placed under a large chestnut tree, where lay three of our horse Guards groaning with pain. I sat down and enquired of one his ailing.

'Oh, sir,' said the poor fellow, 'I'm cut all to pieces. Both of my collar bones are divided.'

The other was insensible. Another presently came up with his coat and shirt open, doubled up, and I saw he was supporting his bowels from a shocking gash in the belly. The battle was heard all round and I fancied a little dismay appeared by the bustle and hurry.

After tarrying five or ten minutes in this Garden, a Gens d'arme came up and asked me what was in my haversack and ordered a foot soldier to give it him, and taking out my German pipe enquired its use; but, doubting affectedly its utility, put it in his pocket swearing 'twas a suspicious utensil.

Two foot soldiers then ordered me to march and, one before and the other behind me, conducted me across the fields through the fighting lines.

As I went through one enclosure a tall Cuirassier, reeling on his horse in the third stage of intoxication, drove up, swearing he'd do for me, which he undoubtedly would have done had not an officer cried out eagerly '*Qu'est que tu va's faire, f.?*' He curbed in his beast with evident reluctance.

We now walked further back from the scene of action and the artillery grew fainter and fainter.

On passing a farm house a woman thrust her fist in my face, exclaiming, 'Ah, dog! You are the cause of this blood-shed.' But a soldier instantly *lui flanqua un soufflet*, with 'What have you to do with politics?'

It now grew dark and ideas of escape began to arise in my mind. But I was not certain of the fate of the day, so we marched until we again reached the high road, and I instantly knew the day was ours by the hurry and tumult visible. Discipline was thrown down and all ranks were levelled. The epaulette was jammed against the musket, and the soldier despised the late imperious commander. Artillery, Cavalry and infantry were jostled together and the road was choaked up with hurry and disorder.

One may fancy the respect paid to a trudging, skulking, unhappy Englishman. One fellow had the insolence to throw his knapsack at my back and endeavour to fasten it to my breast. But I threw it in the mud and lucky it was the horses feet prevented his picking it up instantly or I should have paid dearly for the act.

My guard in front, turning round after an hour's walk, asked me if I wanted to drink, and advised me to dip my cap in some tubs as I passed, which I did and found the liquid was brandy, and I drank it so largely that I became stupid.

The flour was strewed in the road like snow on the Ground to prevent our pursuing army reaping the harvest and the waste was shameful.

Meantime the road became jammed and the utmost consternation ensued. For fear of the conquerors, my two guards took me into a small farmyard on the left, full of dung, on which we rested. Here, free from observation, the fellows whispered together, and one coming said, 'Have you money?'

'No.'

'Give me those epaulettes.'

Now the brandy being in my head I foolishly refused and the fellow behind seized me by the arms and pinioned me to the ground with his knee on my chest, while the other tore off my wings with the lace from my coat. He then pulled off my boots and stockings which he put on, throwing his own shoes over the rails. They then urged me on with the bayonet.

Nothing could equal the pain I felt in walking barefooted for the first time. Every stone I trod on lacerated the bottom of my feet and the torture was acute.

We suddenly came to a plain strewed with naked bodies and I was forced to keep outside the road. The multitude was so thronged I felt a temporary relief to my feet in treading on through soft jellied lumps of inanimate flesh. The French assured me they were all Prussians and I found it was the plain of Fleurus where the war began on the 15th under Blücher.

The night was clear and the moon was nearly full. The men in armour had thrown over themselves their flowing cloaks of a blanket color, and not a word was heard in the crowd but swearing and wrangling now and then. We moved on in this manner for hours, surly and dissatisfied. I saw one carriage in the crowd, but no baggage or stores so plentiful in an English Army.

At length my guards, quite exhausted, went into a field on the left of the road and sat down. Here I remained half an hour and felt feverish. My head ached violently from the wound and I felt the blood was clotted and coagulated, for I was constrained to walk with head bare as well as my feet. The quantity of brandy I had swallowed had caused a parching thirst; and looking round for a ditch I fancied by the moon light I saw a puddle between us and the road. So scooping it up with my hand I swallowed the liquid and found it was horse's urine. So nauseous and disgusting was the taste it produced an instantaneous nausea with a violent reaching, and I discovered a speedy antidote for the sensation by sucking the lining of my military Cap, moist with the spirit it had so recently held.

We marched the whole night and enter'd Charleroi at morning twilight. Here at the entrance, my two guards lay on the heaped up ruins of a delapidated house and fell asleep exhausted, while I sat shrivelled up with cold and misery, my feet black with dirt and bruises, viewing the passing troops, pale with fatigue and exertion, entering the town.

A Grenadier of the Imperial Guard sat himself by me, struck with my unhappy appearance, and, asking me if I spoke French, pulled out a small memorandum book which he told me he took from an Hanoverian Officer whom he had killed and asked me its contents; but I found only the names of his Company. He then took out the pencil and begged of me to write some recommendation of him that it might be of use if ever he fell into our hands so, taking the pencil, I scrawled the following words: 'I Edmund Wheatley, Lieutenant in the German Legion, write this on a bundle of bricks, June 19th 1815 at the entrance of Charleroi in the middle of the retreating French Army. Cold, wounded, barefooted, bareheaded, like a dog in a fair, every one buffets me ad libitum. If the bearer, named Riviere, is in your power, prove to him how differently an Englishman can treat a poor unhappy victim of human instability. Signed, *E Wheatley*.'

The fellow desired me to write it in french. So, cutting the pencil with his sword, I wrote, '*Si Monsr. Riviere, qui porte ceci, tombe entre vos mains je vous prie de lui traiter en frere pour recompenser sa bonne conduite envers le Lieut Wheatley prisonnier a Charleroi, June 19. 1815*.'

Another aged soldier now came up and Riviere said, 'Avez vous quelque chose à donner à ce pauvre enfant?' And he gave me a draught from a horn, but a piece of bread would have pleased me better.

These two men advised me to leave the two sleepers and come with them. But having remarked they had become indifferent lately, and more tired of their duty, my hopes of escape were more sanguine and I refused their kind offer.

A sudden cheering in the town awoke them and they guarded me into the town which I found in tumult and disorder. Presently Buonaparte dashed by with a strong guard with drawn swords clearing the way. But I could not distinguish him in the bustle.

We left the town and followed a retreating body going to the left. On entering a thick wood I saw a body of Belgic prisoners dragging a cannon through the clay, with fellows on horseback beating them with the flat of their swords. They instantly seized me; but I stoutly refused to do it, in spite of the repeated cuts I received on the back and neck. Then one dark, swarthy fellow cries out, '*Tiens! Je lui ferai traveiller*.' So seizing a rope, he fastened it round my two wrists and then to his horse's tail and dragged me forward at a trot amidst the laughter and derision of his comrades. The agony of mind and body I endured is inexpressible.

I ran in this disgraceful plight for a considerable time. At last nature was exhausted and I swooned away.

When I recovered I was laying on the ground, surrounded by a dozen or two of men. An officer of distinction, passing with his servant, asked me who I was and I related the barbarous treatment of the soldiery. Taking a piece of paper from his pocket, his Servant gave him a pen and a horn, and he wrote his name. Over leaf is the identical piece of paper as I received it from his hands.[1]

He then desired me, on arriving at my destination, to write where I was and he would remit some money to me, and rode off.

I now found myself without a Guard in the midst of this conquered

1. The paper is now badly torn and the writing on it illegible.

rabble. On ascending the top of the hill, I looked back and saw at a distance the pursuing army.

At length a Cuirassier of immense stature, seeing me limping and compelled to walk erect from the anguish I endured from the fellow's blow in Charleroi took compassion on me and, pulling his horse in a ditch, desired me to get behind him which I did. And encircling his cuirass with my arms, rode for the space of two hours. The fellow at length ordered me off and offer'd me a two franc piece which he forced me to receive in spite of myself.

I then trudged thro' woods and over heaths for hours. On passing one thick forest among the Cavalry, three or four amused themselves with endeavouring to ride over me. And at last, irritated beyond myself, I burst out into bitter taunts and invectives. Then two of them drew their swords and beat me until I crouched on the ground. One fellow endeavoured to trample on me, but his horse startled and leap'd clean over when I sprang up and ran. A young man pursued me and entering a field of corn waved his sword with *'Venez ici, b.! Venez ici!'*

Seeing no probability of escape I gave a desponding look around and saw in every face sarcasm and deadly irritation. Then, fortunately, espying a cavalier in Green reeling in a perfect state of insobriety, I ran up and looking wishfully in his bloated countenance entreated of him to rescue me from my perilous situation, stating my unguarded helpless condition. Frowning down at me, then at the rascal in the corn, he drew out his enormous sabre and flourishing it over my bare head towards my cruel enemy, hiccup'd out, *'Tiens, villain, si tu ne quitte pas cet homme ci, il ira mal avec toi.'*

Then bidding me lay hold of his stirrup I stuck close to him for a considerable time like Valentine and Orson.[1]

About four o'clock in the afternoon, we entered a small fortress on a hill called Beaumont. The instant I enter'd, two fellows on foot seized me and pushing me into a house forced me down a cellar and shut the door upon me. By the cracks in a board above in the street, through which wine or other articles were lower'd, I perceived I was in company with two fat Prussians, three of our Infantry, a soldier of the 7th Hussars, and one of the Scotch Greys shot through the hand.

1. Valentine and Orson are characters in a French romance, the first English version of which was called *The Historye of the two Valyannte Brethren: Valentyne and Orson.* The brothers were twins abandoned in the forest as babies. One was brought up as a knight, the other grew up in a bear's den and was consequently a wild man until found by his brother, whose servant and companion he became.

Laying down with them, I related how far our troops were in the rere and proposed to fasten the door as well as we could, as no doubt in one hour our own troops would be in the place. I made the same proposal to the Prussians in bad German but they were not unanimous, creating ten thousand difficulties. And all my persuasion had no effect upon them.

I took the poor Scotchman's hand and washed off the blood with spittle and one of the Prussians, having a clasp knife, I eased the pain by letting out some confined blood. Then binding it up with a piece of his shirt, the poor fellow was considerably relieved.

We were shortly taken out and, four behind and four before us with an Officer, we left this town with all its Garrison.

Nothing could exceed the thirst the passing troops expressed for the blood of the two prussians, and I was hoarse in assuring every enquirer they were hanoverian riflemen in our service, which always produced, 'Tant mieux pour eux!'

The French officer over us walked with me and spoke English very correctly. He had been prisoner nine years in England, and was married to an English woman then resident here. I learn'd from him our destination was Avesnes, eleven miles distant, where many of my Countrymen were. I was candid enough to state my determination to escape before the evening, to which he gave no answer. In about an hour I went on one side and lay down in some grass and although the guard endeavourd to urge me on, I stoutly resisted and swore I could not move without a quarter an hour's repose. They left me cursing shockingly.

A Gen's d'arme riding drove me forward, and I marched until the road took a strong descent into a straggling village. Passing a little house I found crowds of soldiers resting. I rested under a tree. The peasant of the house was standing solitary before the door. Being thirsty I was entring the house when he came up to me and was on the point of whispering confidentially to me when looking about he suddenly turned and walked away. I never could understand his meaning, though I've often thought since of it. On entering I found the kitchen thronged with Soldiers quarrelling at the pump. So walking into a little room a thought flashed into my mind like lightening.

I flew upstairs and found myself in a small square room full of broken furniture. Peeping out of window, I saw crowds of frenchmen passing and no one [appeared] to have noticed my absence. So unfastening my Cap from my sash I held it in my left hand and ascended the chimney. Nothing was more unlucky. I jammed myself in in such a manner that I could not for the life and soul of me get higher. My naked feet hung just above the grate. I struggled to get down; [but] it was ineffectual. I endeavoured to bend up my knees but [could not do so] sufficiently to conceal my ankles. My eyes were filled with stale soot and mortar. My right elbow was jammed between the wall and my body; and I was in a state of suffocation from the violent struggles I made to extricate myself from the ludicrous situation. A sudden violent pull at my ankles tore me out, and I fell cover'd with black and filth. Three soldiers [had] by chance come up looking for plunder, and my appearance caused considerable mirth, although I believe they did me a great service. And I walked on with them like a May day sweep.

I walked with the shatter'd remnants of the French Army until past six, when overpower'd I sat down on a bank, the hedges and ditches filled with wearied soldiers. Avesnes was about three mile off.

I now determined to make another endeavour. Seeing some soldiers returning across a small field with some water I went over it, and found [on] the other side of the hedge, a small bye road across which ran a rivulet with a plank to cross it. A soldier was filling a bottle with water and as I stooped down to suck in the liquid the fellow order'd me to wait or he would thrust his bayonet. I let the fellow go and, looking, saw no one watching me. Ten yards behind me was a small house with an elevated garden behind, stoned up somewhat. I flew up the wall like a monkey and, finding the ground sink in a little from the level of the stones, I lay down on my back as flat as possible with a shocking palpitation of the heart.

Finding myself safe I collected my senses as much as possible and framed in my mind a scheme to secure myself from any future apprehension. I lay in this cramped position till about midnight when, stealing down cautiously, I ran to the brook and filled my Cap with water and gained my hiding place unobserved by the crowds passing the other end of the field. I courted sleep but in vain, my anxiety of mind was so strong and my feet and back so painful. The swelling on my head had subsided and only a soreness remained.

20 *June* The rising sun found me in the same state and as I could hear voices pass at the bottom of the wall I was compelled to lay quiet on my back until seven in the evening. At length hearing no

footsteps, no voices, I raised my head and, knowing it impossible for me to lay any longer in this painful position, I groped along the edge of the wall to the back of the garden overlooking the road and saw no one near, but a throng coming down a distant descent of the road.

Before me lay a field of barley up to the calf of the leg. It ascended pretty high and was bounded by a hedge. At top the thick foliage of a forest appeared a little above the hedge, by which I concluded the other side of the hedge was aslant and descended into the forest. I imagined if I gained the hedge safe it would be easy, if pursued, to run down into the forest. By a sudden impulse I cleared the wall, flew across the road, and ran up the field as swift as possible.

I had not reached the middle when a ball whistled by me and, looking, I saw two soldiers in a ditch. One had just fired and the other was presenting. I fell flat in the grass as if shot and recovered my breath by chewing the green barley.

Looking up again I saw the men slowly ascending the field to pick up their game. But I suddenly sprang up and made for the top of the hill. When within ten yards of the hedge I saw two or three heads approaching towards me from the other side, my fancy converted them into Cuirassiers, and seeing the two behind running, I gave it up for lost and, dashing myself head foremost into the hedge, I shut my eyes waiting the result. My heart throbbed so violently I expected it to burst every moment such was the sensation.

Hearing a voice say, '*Qu'est ce que c'est c'a?*' I looked and found two peasants and boy peeping into the hedge. I eagerly enquired if any one was approaching to which they replied two foot soldiers. One whispered, 'Turn your coat and run into the forest,' which I instantly did. But when half way down, I fell and rolled to the bottom into a marsh of reeds through which I waded up to my middle.

A voice from the hill cried out '*Arretez!*' and another ball splashed among the reeds which was the last hostile shot I heard. Then, entering the thickest of the forest, I undrest myself and bathed in a shallow run of clear water. I washed all my clothes of the soot and slime, and, having rinsed them as dry as possible, I clothed myself and dived deeper in for about half an hour. [Then] taking the oil cover [off] my cap I put it over my head. My sash I tore in half and bound over each foot, and laying my hat under my head I placed my feet against a tree and endeavoured to sleep. But I shivered so much from my damp clothes I could not. Night came on and huddling myself into a heap I strived all my power to lose all reflection until day break. But Momus [*Morpheus/Somnus?*] like a woman, the more you entreat the greater the difficulty, but appear to reject, [and] you gain your point.

About midnight it rained, and so close and motionless I lay that the water gather'd in every fold of my clothes, and the least motion produced an instant trickling of the fluid down my cold and almost benumbed limbs. So bewilder'd was my imagination that I had no thought or reflection and I can only compare myself to a man in a trance.

At last twilight appeared and when sufficiently strong to distinguish the foliage I look'd up to my roof and could perceive no stucco work. All was too much fresco and the drops of rain falling so heavily seem'd like so many tears shed by the pitying leaves at sight of my miserable, forlorn, dejected condition.

I began to consider what mode of conduct to pursue and, thinking it best to ensure myself, I limped through the thickets for a considerable time. Having found some trees well entwined at top, I gathered as much grass as Necessary to soften the ground and having tore off a stout cudgel I lay down and entered into a solid cautious and calm meditation. How to live first entered my mind. I had scarcely tasted anything for forty eight hours. Mechanically I felt in all my pockets and found not a crumb. I was so far in the wood that I knew not the way out had I wished, and I knew this Forêt de Soignes to be notorious for its extent. The thought of starving and being shrivelled to a mummy gave me a temporary delirium. But contrasting my situation with that I was in twenty-four hours before calmed my mind, and I amused myself with recalling the events of the last three days. From Waterloo my fancy roved to England, to Soho Square, to Hammersmith, to the white cottage, for I heard Westcroft-place was deserted a few days before the War began.

I knew it was Tuesday because the battle was fought on a Sunday, and I called to mind the night previous to my leaving Hammersmith the first time. I thought just then, if you could but know my condition you would at least pity me, and although I despaired of ever seeing you again, my dear Eliza, I felt even in that hour of acute distress and severe privation, a certain yearning towards you which neither the cold could petrify nor hunger absorb.

Absence, neglect, and misery of miseries had smothered the fire. But a latent spark remained which, like the fire of the vestal virgins burnt slow though sure and was capable of being aroused to a volcano. Many, yea most people would grin at sight of this and call me a fool. But there is such a delight in being guilty of this folly that I am resolved to die an Ass with their permission. I do not pretend to be an Abelard. God forbid! Nor am I a Petrarch, I acknowledge. But if I love sincerely, 'tis nature; if constantly, 'tis virtue; if unselfishly, 'tis commendable; if successfully, 'tis happiness.

I lay all day in this place and about evening strolled about in sight of my hiding place, and having chewed some leaves and drank plentifully of water, I was seized in the night with the most violent gripings of the Stomach and reachings which fortunately produce a stupor and I slept until late next day and felt much refresh'd although [I woke with] an acute pain in the pit of the stomach.

21 June I made up my mind to stroll until I reached some border of the forest, as I concluded the French must be away by that time, and that another night would [so] weaken me as to render my legs useless members of my frame. So forward I went, and about dusk reached the edge of this wilderness.

I felt my heart throb again at sight of the fields and meadows, and thought it prudent to remain concealed until the morning when, *coûte qui coûte*, I would sally out. So chusing my bed among a copse of trees I crawled in like a wild beast and shrugged myself up like a hare in form. The uncertainty of the undertaking next morning kept my eyes open all night and the regular drizzly falling rain chilled my very marrow.

In the middle of the dark and dreary night I heard the bushes giving way and a violent rustling of the branches. The idea of a wolf suggested itself instantly. But it passed on about two yards from my head and I heard no more.

My state of mind and body until day break was really pitiable. My beard was of five days' growth; my feet cut and pricked with flints and thorns; my clothes tattered, damp and chilly. Skulking like an outlaw, rejected and despised by all society in a thicket, in a wood, in an unknown foreign country, unacquainted with the geography or topography of the regions round about, hungry and no prospect of food (as I knew the devestation and misery a conquered army leaves behind them) many dreary leagues to travel alone before I could reach my own countrymen, liable to be murdered by the poor ruined peasants for the injuries they had sustained, such was E. Wheatley's situation on the night of the 21 of June 1815 [Plate 15, *facing p. 64*].

22 June   The long expected morning came. It rained heavily. After sneaking along the outskirts for fifteen minutes, I espied a small house to which I repaired. But notwithstanding the most violent knocking, I could awake no one and I sat on the steps for a full hour then knocked again. No one came; no one heard; no one answered. I endeavoured to force the door, but my strength was exhausted with privation and harrassed with fatigue.

I open'd the little wicket gate of the garden and gathered my hat full of peas [which] I swallowed in a small bower. I afterwards tried the house again; but to no purpose. So walking up a hill overshadowing the house, much like primrose hill near the Regent's Park, I stood on its top and surveyed the whole country beneath. All look'd dreary and uninhabited. Not a creature visible. A quarter of a mile off I perceived the tops of some houses towards which I bent my course.

As I halted along a bye path a peasant suddenly appeared before me. At sight of a human creature I mechanically started. The poor man did the same, '*Donnez moi du pain*,' said I.

'*Ah !Le pauvre enfant*', said the fellow. '*Ah! Le pauvre miserable! Les Français m'ont tous pris.*' And he burst into tears.

I moved on without answering, and just as I was entering the village, a soldier came from behind a house. Never having seen a Prussian with his uniform, a swimming seized my brain and on his questioning me in German I eagerly asked where the French were and [repeated] my old request for some bread. The fellow shrugged up his shoulders with '*Das hab ich nicht*', and passed me.

I then wandered through the village in which I only saw one superannuated woman squatted before her door. All her furniture smashed and thrown into the road with the rest of the people's property.

After walking an hour, I heard a deep groan in a ditch and on going towards it, I saw a poor fellow stretched in the mud at the bottom, and on lifting him up recognized the poor fellow of the Scotch Greys whose hand I had dressed in the cellar at Beaumont on the 19th.

I lifted him up and taking him under my arm, we both groaned on until weary and faint we sat on the edge of a ditch and rested. Here he informed me the French had beaten him, half stripped him, and thrown him in this ditch. I encouraged the poor fellow with assurances that he should share my fortune (2 francs) until we reached some town, which we accomplished to my surprise in the afternoon, by arriving at Beaumont.

The town being full of Prussians, I repaired to Head Quarters and procured some Coffee and dry bread which I shared with my comrade. The Prussian Commander gave me the route written with his own hand.

From Beaumont we went, my poor Comrade and I, to Merbes-le-Chateau, a large village without inhabitants, where we both slept on some straw in an empty room. For in such a state of misery I threw off my superior rank and treated my suffering companion like a brother.

We started next morning, and after a tedious walk till evening descried the village church of Rouvroi. But on reaching it, found a canal between it and us without a bridge to pass. So fastening my clothes on my back, with my sash tied together, I swam over and, dressing on the other side, procured a peasant from the place who shewed my comrade the shallowest part. And he waded through up to his middle.

Here I got his hand dressed by a Prussian Surgeon and bought a loaf and some milk for half a franc.

23 June With great difficulty we reached Mons, a large place, after eleven hours' walk in a state of misery and starvation. Here I assumed my authority as an officer again. The poor soldier I placed in the hospital and gave him a franc and a half which was all I had. And he left me with tears in his eyes and a thousand protestations of gratitude and acknowledgement. The receipt of admission I will also subjoin,[1] to prove the verity of this relation as much as possible. For I know that the incredulity of persons who are not military is very unreasonable and I omit a great many occurrences in order to obtain as much belief as possible, though 'tis very hard indeed.

24 June While wandering about the town like a Piccadilly mendicant I met Birch of Hammersmith who lent me a Napoleon. Dine with him. Bought a pair of stockings and shoes. Got shaved by a woman barber, and marched alone through the Country.

1. This receipt is in the original, but is not reproduced.

29 June Joined my Battalion. [They] would scarcely credit my existence.

*

I have drawn my history to a close. I have complied with your request. I trust you are pleased, Eliza. I have spent many pleasant hours in filling this little book and if Eliza will be pleased with only one single page, the writer is rewarded more than he deserves. For you cannot conceive the fineness and sweetness of that thrill a man feels in his breast when he knows that some word or deed of his, has produced a sensation of joy and delight in the heart of her he prefers to all other women. God Almighty, in his wise and mysterious order of all things, has limited our perception so that we cannot for certain foreknow the consequence of any deed or undertaking. Perhaps, Eliza, in time to come the revision of this little volume will produce sarcasm and dirision. But I have written it to please you. I endeavour to amuse you. I wish I could serve you according to my desires. I cannot Eliza Brookes, now. When I shall be able, God knows only.

You are forbidden to write or hear from me. It is the request of all your Family that you do not see me. Not an individual related to you approves of me. Every dissatisfactory object presents itself. I see numerous difficulties in view. Not a gleam of sunshine. All is chilly and hopeless. I could, if romantically inclined, convert the white Cottage into a massive Castle, with draw-bridge, parapet and turret, giants, dragons, griffins and formidable magicians to contend with ere [I could] gain the Castle entrance and carry off her whose seizure is my wished for prize.

What a melancholy mood I am in and have been all day! Since I saw you yesterday my entire thoughts have been of you and about us.

If ever, my Dear Eliza, the sight of me has found favour with you; if ever the name of Wheatley has been pleasing in your ear, grant me this my most earnest Request – that if ever I bear the weight of your displeasure, it may not be imputed to a depravity of principle, a corruption of morals, or to a turpitude of disposition.

I shall not fatigue your ears with a repetition of vows and solemn promises. Actions speak louder than organs and a most unaccountable change of disposition must take place in me if my future deportment varies from my present resolutions.

Eliza Brookes, have I put on a mask to fascinate your affections? Did I ever under an artificial covering conceal my character or present to you an external to seduce your mind? No, my Eliza, we have been mutually candid and unaffected. We have been faithful and kind. We cannot contend with nature. She is too powerful an opponent to struggle with. The obstacle to our happiness is the lack of money – a very necessary article in this world. When a man is bent on a married life he should have whom he loves. But his mind must be resolved on loving his choice. Ought lucre to be his guide on the search?

I know, Eliza, that at intervals you despair of my further progress and rise in the world. But I am certain, Eliza, I can never be happy in the society of any other woman but you. But are you ever, my dear Friend, in a doubtful mood how to act decidedly about me? I am sure when so solemn and serious a subject as your future destiny in this world occupies your mind, a chaos of bewildering resolutions naturally arises. But pray act according to your judgement. For although I am proud of your friendship for me, in no way do I consider you as bound to me. You are as free and as perfect Mistress in that respect as you were when you recieved my little unvaluable sixpence.

Because, my dear Girl, I wish you (is there any Vanity in the Assertion?) to prefer me (if ever it will be so) for your own sake, not to promote *my* happiness, but [because] you think it will be conducive to your own.

I do not wish my will but your will to be done. If, my Eliza, on mature consideration, your mind should lead you to conclude that it would be more prudent to decline my friendship for worldly reasons, and that more lasting happiness can be obtained, do not suffer our past acquaintance to act as a detainer. For where is my happiness to be found but in the knowledge that yours exists? And if I see you happy, though away from me, think you I shall be miserable, Eliza? This is melancholy talk. But upon my sacred oath I mean it. I hope you will not, while reading this, fancy me romantic; for I do not wish to be thought so, as such a character is deceitful and does not suit the gravity of 25. Here, I do fancy a smile from you. Is it so?

Oh, that the balance may preponderate in my favour! Oh, that Eliza could understand or would credit, every wish, every desire of Wheatley's! Oh, that his means were equal to her merits!

My dearest friend, I will try my utmost to please you.

I would willingly burn this little book. But you will be angry. Well, in years to come (if fate so ordains) read a page or two to me, and if I can calmly hear it without a pang of remorse, sure I shall not be the same Wheatley of 1817.

Good bye, dear. God bless you, my Dear, Dear Eliza. Remember, I swear to be yours only, only Eliza's. *Never think I have forgotten you.*

May 2d. 1817.

Half past 11 O'clock.

Finis.

*

[*When he wrote these final, almost desperate words Wheatley had already been put on half-pay – four shillings a day – due to the disbandment of the King's German Legion in April 1816.*

The story, however, has a happy ending. Eliza succumbed to his entreaties and married him at the church of St Andrew-by-the-Wardrobe on 12 February 1820. Although their first child (Elizabeth Lucy) was born rather quickly on 3 November 1820 it does not appear to have been an enforced or runaway marriage. The witnesses were Elias and Samuel Brookes (her brothers) and one Lucy Bennett.

There were three other children of the marriage – all girls – Jessie, born 3 March 1824, Cornelia Mary, born 10 January 1826 and Malvina Francoise Rosalie, born 20 September 1828.[1]

The French names of this last daughter are accounted for in this way: After being put on half-pay, Wheatley had lived at Wooburn in Buckinghamshire, then (feeling no doubt, that his small income was scarcely enough to live on in England) he had gone abroad, firstly to Bruges, then to Tournai, and finally to Trèves. And it was at Trèves that Eliza's fourth baby was born.

She was such a poor, weak, little thing that the doctor held out small hope of her survival and advised Wheatley to go and fetch a parson to baptize her. Wheatley ran out to find one and on his return discovered that the French nurse, despairing of the child's life, had christened her herself in the Roman Catholic way and had given her her three favourite names. The parents, thankful that their baby was at least still living (she grew up and had a daughter of her own), accepted the fait accompli *and kept the names.*

Edmund Wheatley was still at Trèves when he died on 22 May 1841 in his forty-eighth year.]

1. Public Record Office, W.O. 25/777–778; W.O. 12/11896–11900; War Office Records; Parish Records of St Andrew-by-the-Wardrobe.

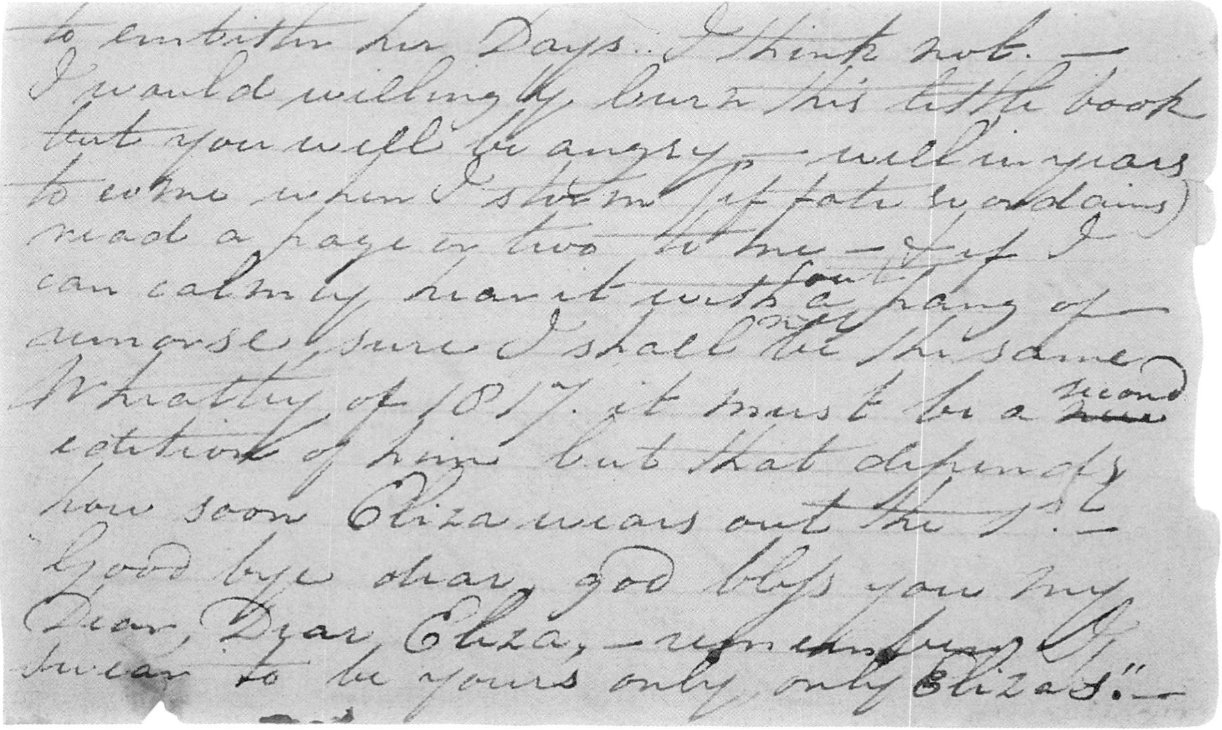

Plate 17 The penultimate page of the diary

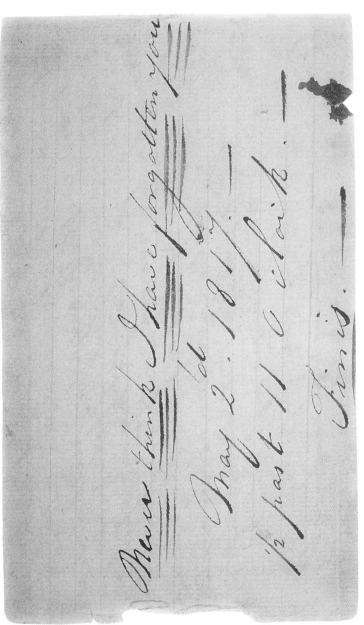

Plate 18 The final page

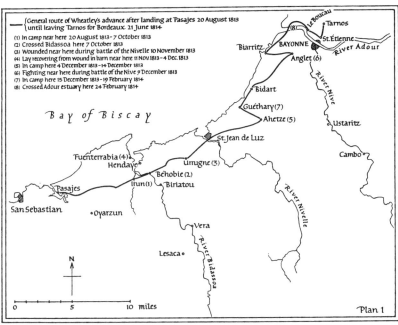

General route of Wheatley's advance after landing at Pasajes 20 August 1813
until leaving Tarnos for Bordeaux. 21 June 1814

(1) In camp near here 20 August 1813 - 7 October 1813
(2) Crossed Bidassoa here 7 October 1813
(3) Wounded near here during battle of the Nivelle 10 November 1813
(4) Lay recovering from wound in barn near here 11 Nov.1813 - 4 Dec. 1813
(5) In camp here 4 December 1813 - 14 December 1813
(6) Fighting near here during battle of the Nive 9 December 1813
(7) In camp here 15 December 1813 - 19 February 1814
(8) Crossed Adour estuary here 24 February 1814

Bay of Biscay

Le Boucau
Tarnos
(8)
St. Étienne
River Adour
Biarritz
BAYONNE
Anglet (6)
River Nive

Bidart
Guéthary (7)
Ahetze (5)
Ustaritz
St. Jean de Luz
Cambo
Fuenterrabia (4)
Hendaye
Urrugne (3)
Behobie (2)
Biriatou
Irun (1)
Pasajes
River Nivelle
San Sebastian
Oyarzun
Vera
Lesaca
River Bidassoa

N

0   5   10 miles

Plan 1

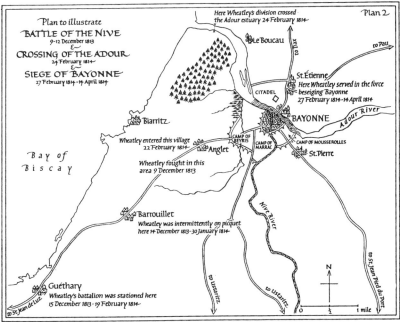

Plan 2

Plan to illustrate
BATTLE OF THE NIVE
9-12 December 1813
&
CROSSING OF THE ADOUR
24 February 1814
&
SIEGE OF BAYONNE
27 February 1814 - 14 April 1814

Here Wheatley's division crossed
the Adour estuary 24 February 1814

Le Boucau
to Dax
to Pau
St. Étienne
Here Wheatley served in the force
besieging Bayonne
27 February 1814 - 14 April 1814
CITADEL
BAYONNE
Adour River
Biarritz
Wheatley entered this village
22 February 1814
CAMP OF BEYRIS
CAMP OF MARRAC
CAMP OF MOUSSEROLLES
Anglet
St. Pierre
Bay of Biscay
Wheatley fought in this
area 9 December 1813
Barrouillet
Wheatley was intermittently on picquet
here 14 December 1813 - 30 January 1814
Nive River
to Ustaritz
to Ustaritz
to St. Jean Pied du Port
Guéthary
Wheatley's battalion was stationed here
15 December 1813 - 19 February 1814
to St. Jean de Luz

N

0   ½   1 mile

91

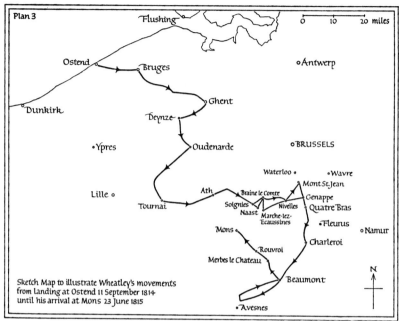

Plan 3

Flushing

0   10   20 miles

Ostend   Bruges   Antwerp

Dunkirk   Ghent   Deynze

Ypres   Oudenarde   BRUSSELS

Lille   Ath   Braine le Comte   Waterloo   Wavre
                                                Mont St.Jean
Tournai   Soignies   Nivelles   Genappe
           Naast   Marche-lez-   Quatre Bras
                     Ecaussines   Fleurus
           Mons   Charleroi   Namur
                   Rouvroi
Merbes le Chateau

Sketch Map to illustrate Wheatley's movements
from landing at Ostend 11 September 1814
until his arrival at Mons 23 June 1815

N

Beaumont

Avesnes

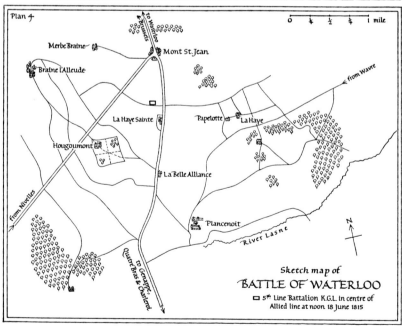

Plan 4

0   ¼   ½   ¾   1 mile

to Waterloo & Brussels

Merbe Braine   Mont St.Jean

Braine l'Alleude   from Wavre

La Haye Sainte   Papelotte   La Haye

Hougoumont

from Nivelles   La Belle Alliance

Plancenoit   River Lasne

N

to Genappe, Quatre Bras & Charleroi

Sketch map of
BATTLE OF WATERLOO
□ 5th Line Battalion K.G.L. in centre of
Allied line at noon 18 June 1815

92

Index

Index

King's German Legion—*(cont.)*
1); punishments in, 11; split into two brigades, 14; at battle of the Nivelle, 14–17, 25; at battle of the Nive, 26–8; anxious to return home, 29; at Adour crossing, 38–40; storm St Etienne, 41–4; casualties at Bayonne, 28 Feb. 1814, 44; Wellington's dispatch, 44–5; warned of attack by Bayonne garrison, 49; losses at Bayonne, 13/14 April 1814, 50; non-German troops disbanded, 55; Wellington's confidence in, xi, 62; at Waterloo, 62–71; disbanded, 1816, 88
1st Light Battalion, K.G.L., xv, 3, 6, 9, 14, 38
2nd Light Battalion, K.G.L., xv, 3, 6, 14, 38, 63
1st Line Battalion, xv, 14, 25, 41
2nd Line Battalion, xv, 9, 14, 16, 25
5th Line Battalion, ix, xv, 1, 2, 6, 14, 16, 25, 26, 27, 38, 41, 44, 47, 48, 50, 55, 56, 62, 63, 65, 66, 68, 69, 70, 85
1st Regiment of Dragoons, xiv

Labouheyre, 53
La Haye Sainte, 63, 68, 71
Le Boucau, 40, 46, 53
Lesaca, xv, 9
Leval, General, 26, 37, 40
Linsingen, Lt.-Colonel William, Baron, 62, 68, 69, 71

Maitland, Colonel Peregrine, 14
Marausin, General, 37
Marche-lez-Ecaussines, 59
Maucomble, General, 40
Maucune, General, 3
Merbes-le-Chateau, 85
Mons, 85
Mont St Jean, 61, 62, 63, 72

Naast, 59
Napoleon, xiv, xvi, 10, 30, 36, 37, 47, 56, 58, 59, 62, 65, 68, 77
Ney, Marshal, Duc d'Elchingen, Prince de la Moscowa, 58, 59, 68
Nive, River, 25, 26, 27, 28, 50
Nivelles, 61
Nivelle, River, 3, 6, 14, 25

Ompteda, Lt.-Colonel Christian, Baron

von, xii, xiii, 5, 16, 17, 28, 35, 38, 41, 42, 62, 68, 69, 70
Orange, William, Prince of, 63, 66, 68, 69, 70, 71
Orthez, 47
Ostend, 56
Oudenaarde, 57
Oyarzun, 19

Pakenham, Major-General Hon. Sir Edward, 31, 44
Pamplona, xv, xvii, 10
Pasajes, 1
Pauillac, 54
Peyrehorade, 37

Quatre Bras, 59, 60

Reille, General Honoré, 37, 40
Rhine, 37
Roncesvalles, 3
Rouvroi, 85

St Etienne, 41, 44, 45, 47, 50
St Jean de Luz, 3, 6, 15, 25, 27, 29, 32, 34, 36, 38
St Pierre, 28
St Vincent, 53
Sambre, River, 59
San Sebastian, xv, xvii, 1
Socoa, 38
Soignies, 59
Somerset, Major-General Lord Edward, 65
Somerset, Colonel Lord Fitzroy, 65
Somerset, Captain Lord John, 69
Sorauen, xviii
Soult, Marshal, Duc de Dalmatia, xvi, 3, 15, 26, 27, 28, 37, 40, 47
Stopford, Major-General the Hon. Edward, xv

Tagus, River, 64
Tarnos, 1, 40, 51, 53
Taupin, 37
Thouvenot, General, 40, 47
Toulouse, 47
Tournai, 57, 58, 88

Urrugne, 3, 6, 7, 15, 17
Urtubia, 6
Ustaritz, 26
Uxbridge, Lieut.-General, the Earl of, 65